AF324017

Uses and Misuses of
Anti-Dumping Provisions
in World Trade

PUBLISHED BY
ACADEMIC FOUNDATION
IN ASSOCIATION WITH

Liberty Institute
New Delhi

Read more about Liberty Institute
on the last page of this book

**Rajiv Gandhi Institute for
Contemporary Studies**
New Delhi

Read more about RGICS
on the last page of this book

THE EDITORS:

Bibek Debroy is Director of the Rajiv Gandhi Institute for Contemporary Studies (RGICS), Rajiv Gandhi Foundation, New Delhi. He is a professional economist and was educated in Presidency College (Calcutta), Delhi School of Economics and Trinity College (Cambridge). He has worked at Presidency College (Calcutta), Gokhale Institute of Politics and Economics (Pune), Indian Institute of Foreign Trade (Delhi), National Council of Applied Economic Research (Delhi) and as Consultant, Department of Economic Affairs, Ministry of Finance, Government of India. He was also the Director for a project known as LARGE, set up by the Ministry of Finance and UNDP to examine legal reforms. He is the author and editor of several books, papers and popular articles and is also Consulting Editor with Business Standard. Bibek Debroy's special interests are international trade (in particular the WTO), law reform and the political economy of liberalisation in India. He has been listed in many bibliographies and has been a member of several government committees.

Debashis Chakraborty is Research Associate at the Rajiv Gandhi Institute for Contemporary Studies, New Delhi. He has worked on trade policy issues and Indian economic development. He is a Doctoral Scholar at the Centre for International Trade and Development Studies, Jawaharlal Nehru University (JNU), New Delhi.

Uses and Misuses of
Anti-Dumping
Provisions in World Trade

A CROSS-COUNTRY PERSPECTIVE

Editors

Bibek Debroy
Debashis Chakraborty

Academic Foundation

NEW DELHI

First published in 2006
by :

ACADEMIC FOUNDATION
4772-73 / 23 Bharat Ram Road, (23 Ansari Road),
Darya Ganj, New Delhi - 110 002 (India).
Phones : 23245001 / 02 / 03 / 04.
Fax : +91-11-23245005.
E-mail : academic@vsnl.com
www : academicfoundation.com

in association with :

Liberty Institute, New Delhi
www.libertyindia.org

and :

Rajiv Gandhi Institute for
Contemporary Studies,
New Delhi

Uses and Misuses of Anti-Dumping Provisions in World Trade :
A Cross-Country Perspective
Editors: Bibek Debroy and Debashis Chakraborty

ISBN 81-7188-511-X

Typeset by Italics India, New Delhi.
Printed and bound in India.

CONTENTS

**1. Anti-Dumping Protectionism in India:
A Critical Study**

Introduction
Trends at WTO
Substantial Dumping Issues at WTO
Dumping Cases in India
Anti-Dumping Initiations Against India
Conclusion

**2. The Rhetoric and Reality of
U.S. Anti-Dumping Law**

Introduction
Missing the Target
Flawed Methodologies
Examining the Case Record
Market Distortions Assumed, Not Proven
Conclusion

3. Anti-Dumping in the European Union

Introduction
The Economics of Anti-Dumping
Anti-Dumping Policy and Actions in the European Union
The European Union and Anti-Dumping

List of Tables and Figures

TABLES

FIGURES

Acronyms

AB	Appellate Body
AD	Anti-Dumping
ADA	Anti-Dumping Agreement
ADD	Anti-Dumping Duties
ATC	WTO Agreement on Textiles and Clothing
CESTAT	Customs, Excise & Service Tax Appellate
DDA	Doha Development Agenda
DGAD	Directorate General of Anti-Dumping & Allied Duties
DOC	United States Department of Commerce
DSB	Dispute Settlement Body
FDI	Foreign Direct Investment
GATT	General Agreement on Tariffs and Trade
ITC	International Trade Commission
MNEs	Multinational Enterprises
MTN	Multilateral Trade Negotiation
NIEs	Newly-Industrialising Economies
NME(s)	Non-Market Economy(ies)
NTB	Non-Tariff Barrier
QRs	Quantitative Restrictions
SSIs	Small Scale Industries
USITC	U.S. International Trade Commission
VAT	Value Added Tax
WTO	World Trade Organisation

Contributors

Bibek Debroy is Director, Rajiv Gandhi Institute for Contemporary Studies, Rajiv Gandhi Foundation, New Delhi. He has authored/ edited several books, papers and popular articles and is also Consulting Editor, *Business Standard.*

Brink Lindsey is Vice President for Research at the Cato Institute in Washington, D.C., and the Director of the Center for Trade Policy Studies at the Institute. Lindsey has written and spoken widely on international economic issues at various forums. He is also an attorney with extensive experience in international trade regulation.

Daniel Ikenson is a Trade Policy Analyst at the Center for Trade Policy Studies, Cato Institute in Washington, D.C. Ikenson has focused on a variety of trade topics, although his research emphasis has been on the subject of anti-Dumping reform.

Debashis Chakraborty is Research Associate at the Rajiv Gandhi Institute for Contemporary Studies, New Delhi. He has worked on trade policy issues and Indian economic development. He is a Doctoral Scholar at the Centre for International Trade and Development Studies, Jawaharlal Nehru University (JNU), New Delhi.

Fredrik Erixon is the Chief Economist of the Swedish think-tank Timbro. He has written extensively on trade, development and international economics and his new book on post-war international political economy, *Quid Pro Quo. Aid, Bretton Woods, Bankruptcy,* will be published in late 2005.

K.D. Raju is Assistant Director, Amity Centre on WTO and Lecturer at Amity Law School, New Delhi. He is also a Doctoral Scholar at the Centre for Studies in Diplomacy, International Law & Economics, Jawaharlal Nehru University (JNU), New Delhi.

Yuefen Li is Senior Economic Affairs Officer in the Division on Globalisation and Development Strategies at UNCTAD, Geneva. She is also a guest professor at Tsinghua University, China. Li has written extensive on trade policy issues.

Introduction

BIBEK DEBROY

The General Agreement on Tariffs and Trade (GATT) was set up in 1947 and sought to liberalise world trade through a series of multilateral trade negotiation (MTN) rounds. From 1 January 1995, GATT was subsumed under the WTO (World Trade Organisation), following the Uruguay Round (1986-94) of negotiations. Since January 1995, five WTO Ministerial Meetings have been held. The Fourth Ministerial in Doha in 2001 was important, because it launched the Doha Development Agenda (DDA), with an initial deadline of January 2005, that couldn't be adhered to. The Sixth Ministerial will be held in Hong Kong in December 2005 and will effectively become a mid-term stock-taking for DDA, apart from fixing deadlines for completion.

The Ministerial Declaration that launched the DDA didn't contemplate any major changes to the anti-dumping agreement. Under the head of WTO Rules, it stated, "In the light of experience and of the increasing application of these instruments by Members, we agree to negotiations aimed at clarifying and improving disciplines under the Agreements on Implementation of Article VI of the GATT 1994 ....while preserving the basic concepts, principles and effectiveness...and taking into account the needs of developing and least-developed participants. In the initial phase of the negotiations, participants will indicate the provisions, including disciplines on trade distorting practices, that they seek to clarify and improve in the subsequent phase." Had the Fifth Ministerial in Cancun in 2003 not failed, there would have been some mid-term stock-taking of these negotiations. At Doha, there was also a Ministerial Declaration on implementation-related issues and concerns. This stated, "The Ministerial Conference agrees that investigating authorities shall examine with special care any application for the initiation of an anti-dumping investigation where an investigation of the same product from the same member resulted in a negative finding within the 365 days prior to the filing of the application and that, unless this pre-initiation examination indicates that circumstances have changed, the investigation shall not proceed. Recognises that, while Article 15 of the Agreement on the Implementation of Article VI of the General Agreement on Tariffs and Trade 1994 is a mandatory provision, the modalities for its application would benefit from clarification. Accordingly, the Committee on Anti-Dumping Practices is instructed, through its working group on Implementation, to examine this issue and to draw up appropriate recommendations within twelve months on how to operationalise this provision. Takes note that Article 5.8 of the Agreement on the Implementation of Article VI of the General Agreement on Tariffs and Trade 1994 does not specify the time-frame to be used in determining the volume of dumped imports, and that this lack of specificity creates uncertainties in the implementation of the provision. The Committee on Anti-Dumping Practices is instructed, through its working group on Implementation, to study this issue and draw up recommendations within 12 months, with a view to ensuring the maximum possible predictability and objectivity in the application of time frames. Takes note that Article 18.6 of the Agreement on the Implementation of Article VI of the General Agreement on Tariffs and Trade 1994 requires the Committee on Anti-Dumping Practices to review annually the implementation and operation of the Agreement taking into account the objectives thereof. The Committee on Anti-Dumping Practices is instructed to draw up guidelines for the improvement of annual reviews and to report its views and recommendations to the General Council for subsequent decision within 12 months."

The origins of anti-dumping legislation can be traced back to the nineteenth century, when the European sugar industries appealed to their respective governments for protection against sugar being dumped at unfairly low prices. In 1902, there was a formal agreement on anti-dumping. Canada adopted the first anti-dumping law in 1904 (there was an earlier version in the last decade of the nineteenth century), followed by other European countries and then the United States in 1916.[1] The US law, modified in 1921, and the Canadian one, formed the basis for the original GATT article (Article VI) on anti-

---

1. This had a clause that predatory intent should exist. The GATT/WTO anti-dumping agreement requires no such proof of predatory intent to drive out competition.

dumping in 1947.[2] Subsequently, codes on anti-dumping were developed during the Kennedy Round (1962-67) and Tokyo Round (1973-79) of MTNs. For example, the Tokyo Round code (which came into force on 1 January 1980) elaborated on Article VI, specifying the basis for imposition, collection and duration of anti-dumping duties and allowing for negotiated agreements, known as price undertakings, between relevant parties. But the Kennedy and Tokyo Round codes were not binding on all GATT members; they were open to signature by those countries that wished to do so. They were plurilateral agreements, not multilateral ones. Unlike these, the Uruguay Round (1986-94) anti-dumping agreement is a multilateral agreement and is binding on all GATT or WTO members. The text of this anti-dumping agreement is included in this volume.

It is a myth that the GATT/WTO system is only about free trade. Plenty of exemptions to free trade principles are permitted. The anti-dumping agreement is one such exemption. The GATT/WTO system does not prohibit dumping, defined as exporting a product at lower than its "normal value." Normal value is defined as the price, "in the ordinary course of trade, for the like product when destined for consumption in the exporting country." Thus, the normal value is a fair selling price in the domestic market of the exporting country, provided that a like product sold in the domestic market can be found. If there are no sales of a like product in the domestic market, or if the volume of these sales are insignificant, two other methods can be used for determining normal value. The first option is to compare the export price with the export price of a like product to a third country. If there are no reasonable export prices for comparison, a second option is to construct normal value on the basis of cost of production in the country of origin, with mark-ups for administrative, selling and general costs and profits. Having done all this, one may or may not have established dumping. But as mentioned above, dumping *per se* is not GATT/WTO incompatible. For action to taken against dumping, one has to in addition establish injury to domestic industry. A causal link between the act of dumping and the act of injury must also be established and if this link is established, anti-dumping duties can be imposed.

---

2. Article VI stated, 'the contracting parties recognise that dumping, by which products of one country are introduced into the commerce of another country at less than the normal value of the products, is to be condemned if it causes or threatens material injury to an established industry in the territory of a contracting party or materially retards the establishment of a domestic industry.'

An anti-dumping investigation can be started only if there is a written complaint on behalf of domestic industry. This complaint can be considered if a significant share of domestic producers supports the complaint. There are two complementary criteria to define "significant." The application must be supported by producers who account for at least 50 per cent of the total output and producers supporting the complaint must account for at least 25 per cent of output produced by producers who are not indifferent to the issue. Unsubstantiated complaints must be rejected. Investigation will also be terminated if the margin of dumping is minimum or *de minimis*, defined as less than 2 per cent, expressed as a percentage of the export price. Investigations will also be terminated if the volume of dumped imports from any country accounts for a less than 3 per cent market share of imports of the like product in the importing country, unless such exporters collectively account for more than 7 per cent of imports. There is also a sunset clause on anti-dumping duties. Unless revalidated through a fresh review, anti-dumping duties will expire five years from the date of imposition.

The Uruguay Round anti-dumping agreement represents an improvement on the Kennedy and Tokyo Round codes, especially on injury and establishing the causal link between dumping and injury. The WTO's website has a synopsis of the anti-dumping agreement and highlights its plus points.

However, there are plenty of minuses as well. First, there is quite a bit of arbitrariness in determining what is "like" product. If an exported product is not identical to a product sold in the domestic market, case-by-case cost-based adjustments are made to the sales price in the domestic market and this offers scope for further arbitrariness. Second, the domestic sales price can be considered if it is "in the ordinary course of trade." Thus, low prices charged for sales in the domestic market can be ignored on grounds of these not being arm's length transactions and, therefore, not in the ordinary course of trade. This serves to jack up the domestic sales price and makes it easier to prove dumping. Alternatively, it can be argued that such sales are below the per unit average cost of production and should be disregarded. Third, if the normal value is constructed, there are complicated cost calculations and allocations to be made, for instance, between sales in the domestic market and the export market. If there is a conflict between accounting practices in the exporting country and the importing country, investigating authorities typically follow accounting practices in the importing country. Apart from the fact that Indian exporters often do not maintain account books at all, or do not maintain separate accounts for exports and domestic sales, the inefficient and non-transparent indirect tax structure makes it difficult to allocate costs appropriately. If such account books are not available, normal value can be constructed on the basis of cost for the same general category of products, those for other exporters or producers or "any other reasonable method." Each of these offers further scope for arbitrariness. Incidentally, if required information on costs is not forthcoming from exporters, investigations can be undertaken on the basis of "best information." Fourth, comparison of the export price and sales price in the domestic market requires exchange rate conversions, and exchange rate fluctuations can influence the comparison. The agreement stipulates that the exchange rate on the date of sale should be considered. But the date of sale can be the date of contract, purchase order, order confirmation or date of invoice, and depending on which is chosen, comparisons may differ. Fifth, to obtain the margin of dumping, the weighted average normal value should be compared with a weighted average of export prices, or normal value should be compared with the export price on transaction-to-transaction basis. But under certain circumstances, the weighted average normal value can also be compared to the export price for a specific transaction and this can result in higher dumping margins. In addition, in computing a weighted average dumping margin, the agreement is unclear about how negative dumping should be treated. Sixth, if preliminary investigations establish dumping and injury, exporters may give voluntary price undertakings to revise prices or cease exports at dumped prices. In practice, such price undertakings are anything but voluntary. Seventh, the agreement is unclear about whether the amount of anti-dumping duty should be equal to the margin of dumping or less (margin of injury, say). Anti-dumping duties cannot, however, exceed the margin of dumping. Eighth, anti-dumping duties are product and source specific. They can, therefore, be circumvented by changing the customs tariff classification, slightly altering the goods or completing a part of the production process in the country of import or a third country. The anti-dumping agreement has virtually nothing to say on such circumvention. Ninth, in instances of dumping, users of the dumped product (industrial users or final consumers) benefit from lower prices. These represent welfare gains from dumping. The Uruguay

Round anti-dumping agreement, for the first time, stipulates that such users should be consulted. But this evidence is only on dumping, injury and causality, not in terms of welfare gains that accrue to consumers. Apart from such welfare losses, given the present provisions of the anti-dumping agreement and clauses that allow subjectivity, it is the easiest thing in the world to prove dumping. But interpreted literally, since all other relevant factors must be excluded, it is virtually impossible to demonstrate injury or causality. In operational terms, most countries, therefore, establish dumping and have a perfunctory proof of injury or causality.

Here is another quote that highlights the minuses. This quote, so to speak, is the Ministry of Commerce's (Government of India) official line on anti-dumping, and is reproduced from the newsletter on the Ministry of Commerce website.[3] While this is from a 1999 version of the newsletter, the thrust of the argument hasn't changed since then. "Another instance is provided by Article 15 of the Agreement on implementation of Article VI of the General Agreement on Tariffs and Trade 1994, which relates to anti-dumping. ... However, we find that anti-dumping measures are being virtually used as weapons by certain developed countries to deny access to the products of developing countries. On the same commodity, anti-dumping action has been repeatedly initiated by certain developed countries. This has created instability and unpredictability in the market, which militates against basic GATT principles. It is vitally important to lay down clear guidelines for making sure that the provision in Article 15 is translated into practice. Some areas where special and differential treatment can be considered for exports from developing country members are enumerated below: a) A *de minimis* dumping margin limit of 2 per cent of export price has been prescribed and no anti-dumping duty can be imposed if the dumping margin is below this threshold limit. This *de minimis* limit is the same for exports from developing as well as from developed countries. Many of the export products of developing countries are produced by labour intensive small and medium enterprises. Imposition of anti-dumping duties, or even the threat of imposition of such duties has a serious adverse effect on the functioning of such units. As a consequence, there is fall in production, heavy unemployment, decline in incomes and increase in poverty levels. In view of the high sensitivity of these sectors to any

---

3. See, *India and the WTO*, Vol. 1, No.4 April 1999.

export disruption, the *de minimis* dumping margin of 2 per cent should be enhanced. The level of enhancement in respect of each developing and least developed country should reflect the disadvantage that the industry in such country suffers *vis-à-vis* comparable production in developed countries. For instance, the Federation of Indian Chambers of Commerce and Industry has estimated that the disadvantage suffered by Indian industry by way of differential costs of working capital, financing cost of refund of excise duty, intangible infrastructure costs, sales tax on local bought outs and octroi amounts to approximately 17 per cent. The inherently high prices sometimes maintainable in the domestic market are not sustainable in exports, and the prices of the latter often represent reduced levels of profitability for the exporters. The price differential of 2 per cent presently constituting the *de minimis* dumping margin is unrealistically low. However, the extent of disadvantage would vary from country to country and its assessment could be a cumbersome, contentious issue. Hence, it is better to have an across-the-board *de minimis* which could be prescribed *vis-à-vis* all developing countries to adequately reflect the higher price levels which prevail in such countries. b) Article 5.8 of the Anti-Dumping Agreement presently provides that the volume of dumped imports shall normally be regarded as negligible, if the volume of dumped imports from a particular country is found to account for less than 3 per cent of imports of the like product, unless countries which individually account for less than 3 per cent of the imports of the like product collectively account for more than 7 per cent of the imports into the importing Members. In view of the liberalisation of global trade and in view of the fact that more and more developing countries are entering into what were earlier untapped markets for them; it is necessary to increase these percentages with a view to help developing countries. These percentages should be increased respectively to 7 per cent and 15 per cent in the case of imports from a developing country into a developed country. c) Since, anti-dumping investigations are against specific exporters, the impact of investigations and the resulting duties, if any, are felt by the exporters from developing countries who, more often than not, are very small in size and operations. The cost of defending the interests of the exporters of the developing country Members is also prohibitive and a matter of concern. It is, therefore, important and that investigations should be initiated against developing country members only if the petition has the support of at least 50 per cent of the domestic industry of the developed country Members. Further, no investigation should be initiated for a period of 365 days from the date of finalisation of previous investigation for the same product resulting in non-imposition of duties. However, if it is established by the complainants that the circumstances have changed drastically subsequently to the finalisation of a case, such investigation should be initiated only if it has the support of at least 75 per cent of the domestic industry of the developed country Members. Further, stricter criteria should be applied for such repeated investigation and this should not be less than one year. Guidelines should be established to define the parameters of establishing 'drastic' change of circumstances and the 'stricter criteria' to be applied in such cases. d) Article 9.1 of the Agreement allows the investigating authorities to impose anti-dumping duties where all requirements for imposition have been fulfilled. This Article further states that it is desirable that the duty be less than the margin of dumping if such lesser duty would be adequate to remove the injury to the domestic industry. It is matter of concern that a large number of developed countries, who also happen to be active users of the mechanism, apply duties to the full extent of the margin of dumping. While the Agreement does not make it obligatory for the investigating authorities to follow the 'lesser duty rule' the application of duties to the full extent of dumping margins invariably leads to higher level of protection to the domestic industry, which is in excess of the duty required to negate the injury caused to their domestic industry. It would be appropriate, therefore, to have a special provision that the application of the lesser duty rule be made mandatory when a developed country member is investigating the alleged dumped imports from a developing country member. In addition, norms and criteria should be established to operationalise the 'lesser duty' route in terms of 'adequacy' to remove 'injury'. e) The Agreement of Anti-Dumping has severely limited the role of panels in disputes relating to Anti-Dumping. Article 17.6 lays down that if the panel finds that the authorities have established and evaluated facts properly, objectively and without bias, it shall not overturn the conclusion reached by the authorities even though, on the basis of same facts, the panel itself would have decided differently. Since, developed countries are increasingly resorting to the use of anti-dumping duties against developing countries, it is necessary that what is applicable to disputes relating to other covered agreements is made applicable to disputes relating to anti-dumping."

In sum, the arguments are the following. Developed countries have been restoring to protectionism and this surfaces through anti-dumping investigations, often through a fresh round of anti-dumping investigations on the same product. Policy substitution is understandable in a situation where tariffs are disciplined, since protectionism will not go away. There must be special and different treatment for developing countries. The *de minimis* margin must be increased (for developing countries) and so must the figure for "negligible" imports from developing countries. If investigations are launched against developing countries, the percentage of domestic industry that supports the application must be increased. The lesser duty rule must be followed. If a dispute settlement panel arrives at a conclusion that is different from the conclusion arrived at by the country imposing anti-dumping duties, the panel must be allowed to overturn the imposition of anti-dumping duties.

From an Indian perspective, the anti-dumping agreement has two angles. First, Indian exporters face anti-dumping investigations abroad. More than the imposition of anti-dumping duties, the process of investigations constitutes a non-tariff barrier (NTB) and impedes Indian exports. A point needs to be made here about the almost universal classification of anti-dumping duties under the head of NTBs, thus, reinforcing the argument that there is policy substitution from protection through tariffs to protection through NTBs. Conceptually, it is not clear why anti-dumping duties should be called NTBs. Duties are price-based measures. Presumably, the argument is that anti-dumping investigations and resultant transaction costs act as NTBs, but this distinction between the two aspects of anti-dumping is rarely made. This angle of anti-dumping has always been important. On this, there are problems in demonstrating costs of production because of the non-transparent nature of the indirect tax system.[4] The complete VAT (value added tax), integrated for goods and services, is a long way off and such problems also occur in the context of the subsidies and countervailing measures agreement. Second, products may be dumped into India. Historically, with high import duties and quantitative restrictions (QRs) on imports, this aspect of dumping was not that important for India. But with reforms, import duties

---

4. There are additional problems of Indian exporters not maintaining proper books of accounts or these not conforming to international accounting standards. If they are maintained, they are not carefully separated into domestic sales and export sales and there is the additional problem of joint production.

have been brought down and QRs have been phased-out, barring those retained on Article XX and XXI grounds. Therefore, dumping into India has also become important. And India has become a major user of anti-dumping investigations, as well as NTBs through standards.[5]

Subject to the negotiations at the Sixth Ministerial in Hong Kong, the DDA does not involve re-negotiation of the anti-dumping agreement, although amendments to the agreement may turn out to be more significant than was contemplated in Doha in 2001. But even if there is such a review, that will be no more than cosmetic, involving greater invocation of special and differential treatment to developing countries and greater general disciplines.

However, there is a deeper point. The anti-dumping agreement is violative of basic free trade principles and needs to be scrapped. On balance, developed countries have lost comparative advantage in goods and have become more protectionist. Conversely, developing countries stand to benefit from greater liberalisation and opening up. While Indian producers of import substitutes tend to lose if anti-dumping action is waived, welfare gains to users will be more than proportionate. In addition, Indian exporters will benefit from removal of non-tariff barriers (NTBs) that anti-dumping investigations amount to. This is a reason why developing countries like India should argue for scrapping of the anti-dumping agreement. Even if the anti-dumping agreement is scrapped, within the GATT/WTO framework, temporary protection to domestic industry against injury is possible through the safeguards agreement, although unlike the anti-dumping agreement, use of the safeguards clause requires compensation to trading partners.

In an ethical sense, dumping cannot be objected to unless it is linked up with predatory policies and anti-trust legislation. For instance, market structures in the domestic market might be monopolistic or oligopolistic, permitting cross-subsidisation of exports. But this underlines entry barriers and distortions that allow such market structures to continue. Alternatively, government policies

---

5. However, care must be taken in comparing data on India's use of anti-dumping investigations. These originate either through WTO, or through India's internal data generation system, although the latter feeds into the former. The classification systems are not the same. For instance, if there is an investigation involving multiple countries, the Indian reporting system classifies this as a single anti-dumping investigation. But in WTO's reporting system, this is counted multiple times, each country counting as a separate investigation.

and non-transparent pricing might permit cross-subsidisation of exports. The issue, thus, is one of competition policy, which will eventually be on WTO's agenda. Globally, if one looks at competition policies, they are based on structure (market shares), conduct (unfair or restrictive trade practices) or performance (price, profitability). Cross-country experiences also suggest that competition policies based on performance rarely work. Nor do competition policies based on structure, unless they involve demonopolisation of public sector monopolies or mergers and acquisitions. Successful competition policies are based on conduct. There exists a parallel there. The anti-dumping agreement has no link with conduct, but is based on prices alone. Therefore, it often taxes efficiency and subsidises inefficiency. If a cross-national competition policy agreement can be worked out through the WTO, the anti-dumping agreement should cease to have any further relevance. This scrapping should not, however, be interpreted as a simple repeal of Article VI. In the absence of Article VI, member countries will have the freedom to adopt whatever rules they desire on anti-dumping and such unilateral action is undesirable. Instead, Article VI needs to be disciplined and linked up to tests for predatory intent through competition policy provisions. Of course, there are problems in implementation. Rare is the case when predatory intent can be demonstrated *a priori*. Established *post facto*, the harm has been done.

While the form that a new Article VI takes can be debated, this is the background against which the five papers included in this volume need to be considered. The five papers (two are from India) are remarkably unanimous in their condemnation of the anti-dumping provisions, with the one on China a little less explicit. The first paper by K.D. Raju highlights some problems with the anti-dumping agreement and then goes on to discuss the Indian case. The point is made that anti-dumping duties often ignore costs suffered by consumers in the process and protect domestic industry, with the latter often representing monopolies. In the second paper, Brink Lindsey and Daniel Ikenson concentrate on the rhetoric and the reality of US anti-dumping law. The point is made that the level playing field or fair competition argument is a red herring. And it is argued that US policies, legitimate under Article VI, have little to do with finding price discrimination or sales below cost. This is bolstered by the argument that even when such pricing evidence is found, that has little to do with market distortions. Not only does US practice of anti-dumping law have little to do with the rhetoric of ensuring a level playing field, it encourages lobbying for protection. The point is that this is sanctioned by the anti-dumping agreement. From the United States, one moves on to the third paper by Fredrik Erixon, on the EU. Although, the background is somewhat different, the finding is no different from the US one. The EU practice has moved away from the original purpose of anti-dumping law and is nothing but a common protectionist measure. China is a major target of anti-dumping investigations, including by India. Yuefen Li's fourth paper attempts to explain why and given that focus, is a less outright condemnation of the anti-dumping agreement, although the loopholes are indeed mentioned. In part, the answer lies in China's export success, despite China not having attracted enough FDI and multinational enterprises (MNEs) so as to jump the anti-dumping agreement, so to speak. This is an important argument and is one not that familiar to the rest of the world. Add to this the point about China's WTO accession protocol, which requires China to be treated, for anti-dumping purposes, as a non-market economy till 2016. This allows deviations and increases the probability of a positive anti-dumping findings. And finally, there is inadequate Chinese legal capacity to defend against anti-dumping investigations. The fifth and final paper by Debashis Chakraborty repeats some of the protectionist and loophole arguments. And then brings in the dispute settlement provisions, by analysing Article by Article, the WTO-incompatibility of anti-dumping practices followed by individual countries. There is particular focus on India. This analysis also permits identification of Articles where the present anti-dumping agreement leaves scope for ambiguity and, thus, enhances the probability of disputes.

Where do we go from where? As mentioned earlier, the DDA contemplates nothing beyond clarifying and improving disciplines. There is consensus across all five papers that this is hardly enough. More substantial change is needed in the anti-dumping agreement. There is perhaps consensus across all five papers that the anti-dumping agreement needs to be dumped, although there is lack of precision about what should be done about Article VI in that eventuality. Given the political economy within the WTO, this first-best solution is unlikely to materialise. But as a second-best, there is enough ammunition in these five papers for the argument that one needs much more than mere clarification and improvement.

1

Anti-Dumping Protectionism in India: A Critical Study

K.D. RAJU

Introduction

Dumping cases are sensitive and a hot topic in the international trading system. Very few countries were the users of this procedure up to the 1980s. During the 1990s, the number of countries using this measure to block imports increased. The establishment of WTO in 1995 and adoption of the WTO agreements, including Article VI (popularly known as the anti-dumping agreement) of the General Agreement on Tariffs and Trade (GATT), changed the scenario. Now the whole regime is controlled by this international agreement. Since the adoption of the WTO anti-dumping agreement (ADA), the number of initiations shot up amazingly all over the world and this kind of protectionism is no longer the monopoly of developed countries now. The trend has shifted towards the developing countries as well. Over the last couple of years, India has emerged as a leader in using this protectionist measure. It is also interesting to note that most of the initiations are against other developing countries. Mostly the imports from a non-market economy like China are targeted.

Internationally the expression "dumping" has been defined differently. In a layman's view, it is sales of goods in the market for a lower price. In anti-dumping law, a product is considered as dumped if its export price is lower than its normal value. The export price and normal value are defined according to the national law of various WTO members after taking into account special situations of that country. A fair comparison between normal value and export price has to be made for finding out the dumping margin. If the dumping margin is more than 2 per cent, anti-dumping duties can be imposed, otherwise it is considered as *de minimis*. Furthermore, existence of dumping is not the sole criteria for imposing anti-dumping duties.

Injury to the domestic industry and a causal relationship between dumping and injury must be established.

In India, anti-dumping cases are of recent origin. This may be due to prevalence of high tariffs on imports for a major part of the nineties. Quantitative restrictions also played a crucial role in preventing dumping of goods into the Indian market. India included anti-dumping provisions in 1985 in its laws, which were amended in accordance with the ADA in 1995. Sections 9A, 9AA, 9B and 9C were included in the Customs Tariff Act, 1975 for that purpose. India initiated its first anti-dumping investigation in 1992.

Trends at WTO

Since the establishment of the WTO in 1995 and up to December 2004, out of the 148 Member countries, 98 Members initiated 2646 investigations. During this period, India initiated 400 investigations and, thus, became the front-runner in this field. US was placed in the second position (354), followed by EU (303), Argentina (192), South Africa (173), Australia (172), Canada (133), China (99), Turkey (89) and Mexico (79).

China is the major victim, with 411 initiations against it between 1995 and December 2004. Korea is in the second position (207),

Figure 1.1

Anti-Dumping Initiations from 1980 to 2004, All Over the World

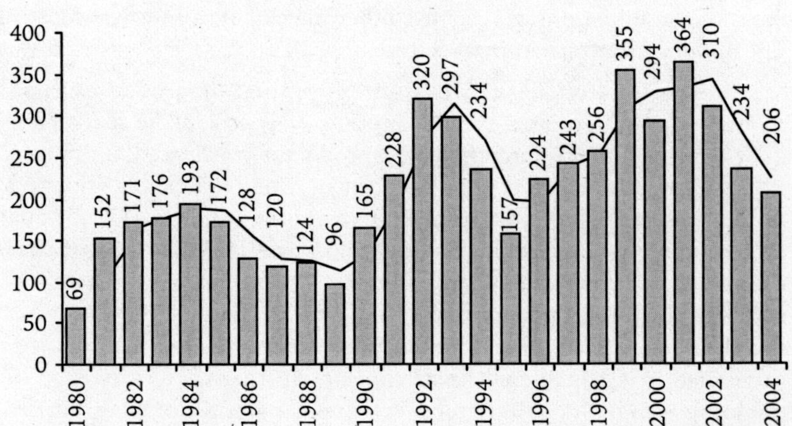

followed by the US (152), Chinese Taipei (146), Japan (118), India (108), Indonesia (107), Thailand (100), Russia (94) and Brazil (80).

Substantial Dumping Issues at WTO

WTO members are quite concerned at the spurt in anti-dumping actions recently. In many cases, the aggrieved Members have approached the WTO dispute settlement body (DSB) for redressal of their grievances. Presently, majority of the cases lodged before the DSB are on the misuse of anti-dumping provisions. Many Members complained about misuse of this provision for partisan and protectionist purposes, the validity of which claim has been substantiated by several decisions of the DSB. In *EU India Bed Linen* case, the Appellate Body (AB) held that the "zeroing" methodology used by EU for calculation of dumping margin is against the ADA provisions. The EU and the US frequently use this methodology. Zeroing methodology eliminates negative dumping margins from the calculation of dumping margin, and always leads to positive dumping margin in calculations. If there are only positive dumping margins, it doesn't make any impact on the calculations, but zeroing of negative dumping margins practised by these countries are problematic.

India is a strong supporter of abolition of the "zeroing" methodology. However, a former Indian Ambassador to WTO admitted that India also have been using this methodology in some of the cases dealt with by the Directorate General of Anti-Dumping & Allied Duties (DGAD), after pressure from particular industry circles. In the *Softwood Lumber* dispute brought by Canada, the WTO Panel held that "the US has violated Article 2.4.2 of the ADA by not taking into account all comparable export transactions when United States Department of Commerce (DOC) calculated the overall margin of dumping as Article 2.4.2 requires that the existence of margins of dumping has to be established for softwood lumber on the basis of a comparison of the weighted-average-normal value with the weighted average of prices of all comparable export transactions, that is, for all transactions involving all types of products under investigation."

It is interesting to note that the EU, proponent of the "zeroing" methodology, approached the DSB against the use of zeroing by the US in 31 different anti-dumping cases. It is clear in the aftermath of the decision in the *EU-India Bed Linen* case that the DSB may also rule against the US in this dispute. However, even after an adverse decision against "zeroing", there is every possibility of arguing in favour of this methodology in individual cases by the US. This is mainly due to the ambiguity in Article 2.4.2 of the ADA. The AB ruled in the *Bed Linen* case that zeroing prevents average-to-average comparisons. The ADA permits individual to average comparisons in certain circumstances. If dumping is calculated otherwise, like average to individual comparisons, there is the possibility of finding dumping. These will be completely ADA consistent. It means, even after the adverse ruling against zeroing, the ambiguity still remains.

Table 1.1

Zeroing

Product Code	Net E.M* Price	Net H.M* Price	Unit Margin	Quantity	Total Value
1	$1.00	$0.50	-$0.50	100	$100
2	$1.00	$1.00	$0.00	100	$100
3	$1.00	$1.00	$0.00	100	$100
4	$1.00	$1.00	$0.00	100	$100
5	$1.00	$1.50	$0.50	100	$100
Total Margin Without Zeroing			$0		
Total Margin Using Zeroing			$50		
Total Value					$500
Final Dumping Margin					10.00%

Source: *www.wto.org*
    * E.M-Export Market, H.M-Home Market.

Back-to-back investigations are another menace faced by the developing countries. In the *EU-India Bed Linen* dispute, EUROCOTTON was unable to manage the required support for its first application in 1994, and the investigation was terminated in 1996. The fact that the second investigation was initiated immediately after 20 days of the termination of the first investigation, shows the misuse of the provisions. An investigation is more effective than actual anti-dumping duties in many cases. This is mainly due to the "chilling effect" and harassment of importers during the investigation process. Therefore, there is an urgent need to induct a new provision in the ADA which prohibits a fresh investigation within one year after the finding of non-dumping in a previous investigation.

Article 15 of the ADA provides for special and differential treatment of developing countries. India claimed this privilege in the *EU-India Bed Linen* dispute. However, EU stated that they considered India's request, but found no other constructive remedies. It has been pointed out that Article 15 is a "soft law" provision within the "hard law" obligations under WTO agreements. The Doha Ministerial Declaration also confirmed the sentiments of developing country members and decided to review this provision.

Article 6.8 and Annex II of the ADA authorises the use of "facts available," when a party refuses access to or does not provide necessary information within a reasonable period of time or when a party significantly impedes the process of investigation. In many cases, this provision is misused by the investigation authorities. In the *United States - Anti-Dumping Measures on Certain Hot-rolled Steel Products from Japan* dispute, the Panel held that the US investigating authorities violated this particular provision of ADA. Provisions are not clear as to under what circumstances the "facts available" provision can be used. In *India-Steel Plate* dispute also, the US authorities rejected the submitted data and took recourse to this provision for a decision in favour of the US steel industry. In this case also, the WTO Panel rejected the argument of the US authorities. There is an urgent need to standardise and simplify the procedures in submitting required trade data.

Dumping Cases in India

The amendment and inclusion of Sections 9A, 9AA, 9B and 9C to the Customs Tariff Act, 1975 was in accordance with the obligations under the ADA. In 1992, India initiated its first dumping investigation on PVC Resin exported from Brazil, Mexico, Korea and the US. Gradually the number of cases increased to 81 in 2002 and then decreased to 21 in 2004. It is interesting to note that out of 400 initiations, only 167 initiations ended in investigations and in 142 cases, final decisions have been made. Preliminary findings are over in 6 cases and 10 cases are pending for final/interim decisions. Only 9 cases have been closed after investigations. This means that only 42 per cent of the applications have ended in investigations and only 5 per cent applications stand closed without imposing any duties.

Between 1992 and 2004, appeals were filed in 63 cases by various interested parties in the Customs, Excise & Service Tax Appellate

Tribunal (CESTAT), out of which, final rulings have been made by CESTAT in 46 cases. Thirty one cases have been decided in favour of the DA, orders of the DA have been modified in 11 cases and in 4, orders have been quashed. During this period, 32 writ petitions have been filed in various High Courts. In 2 cases, matters have been transferred to the Supreme Court and 14 cases are pending for orders. The number of appeals filed in the Supreme Court between 1992 and 2004 is 18. The Supreme Court passed orders in 5 cases and 13 cases are pending for orders by the Supreme Court.

Figure 1.2

Anti-Dumping Initiations by India, 1992-2004

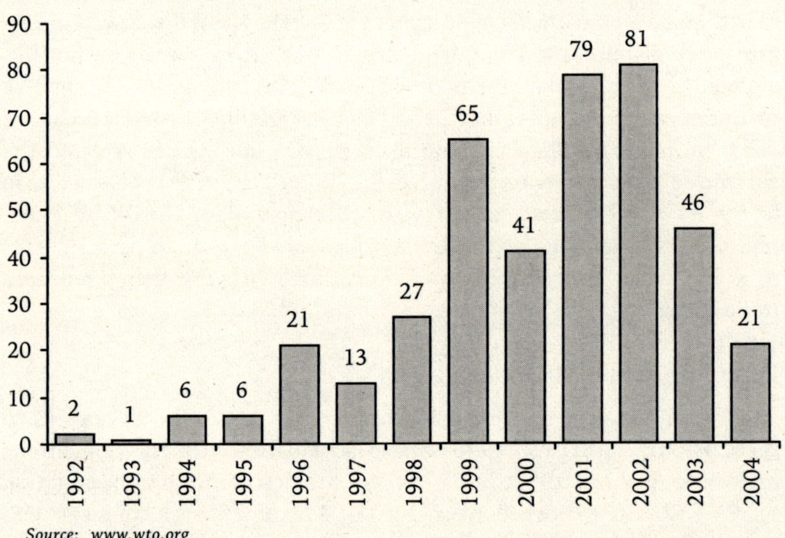

Source: www.wto.org

In India, remedy before the appellate tribunal, the CESTAT is speedier. For circumventing speedy remedy, many petitions are filed before the High Courts (under Article 226 of the Indian Constitution) and Supreme Court of India. The number of cases pending before the High Courts and Supreme Court shows that there is enough scope for improving the pace of dispute resolution in India. This is causing disruptions in trade for the interim period and there is an urgent need to have a special bench of the Supreme Court for this purpose.

Table 1.2

Product-wise Anti-Dumping Initiations by India

WTO Product Category No.	Products	Indian Initiations
I	Live animals; animal products.	
II	Vegetable products.	
III	Animal or vegetable fats and oils and their cleavage products; prepared edible fats; animal or vegetable waxes.	
IV	Prepared foodstuffs; beverages, spirits and vinegar; tobacco and manufactured tobacco substitutes.	
V	Mineral products.	7
VI	Products of the chemical or allied industries.	141
VII	Plastics and articles thereof; rubber and articles thereof.	48
VIII	Raw hide and skins, leather, furskins and articles thereof; saddlery and harness; travel goods, handbags and similar containers; articles of animal gut (other than silk-worm gut).	
IX	Wood and articles of wood; wood charcoal; cork and articles of cork; manufactures of straw, of esparto or of other plaiting materials; basketware and wickerwork.	
X	Pulp of wood or of other fibrous cellulosic material; recovered (waste and scrap) paper or paperboard; paper and paperboard and articles thereof.	6
XI	Textiles and textile articles.	36
XII	Footwear, headgear, umbrellas, sun umbrellas, walking-sticks, seat-sticks, whips, riding-crops and parts thereof; prepared feathers and articles made therewith; artificial flowers; articles of human hair.	1
XIII	Articles of stone, plaster, cement, asbestos, mica or similar materials; ceramic products; glass and glassware.	4
XIV	Natural or cultured pearls, precious or semi-precious stones, precious metals, metals clad with precious metal and articles thereof; imitation jewellery; coin thereof; imitation jewellery; coin.	
XV	Base metals and articles of base metal.	29
XVI	Machinery and mechanical appliances; electrical equipment; parts thereof; sound recorders and reproducers, television image and sound recorders and reproducers, and parts and accessories of such articles.	22
XVII	Vehicles, aircraft, vessels and associated transport equipment.	
XVIII	Optical, photographic, cinematographic, measuring, checking, precision, medical or surgical instruments and apparatus; clocks and watches; musical instruments; parts and accessories thereof.	
XIX	Arms and ammunition; parts and accessories thereof.	
XX	Miscellaneous manufactured articles.	
XXI	Works of art, collectors' pieces and antiques.	
...	Unknown.	

Source: WTO Secretariat, 2005.

As seen from the Table 1.2, India initiated 48 per cent of its total cases against petrochemicals, chemicals and other products. The second category is plastics and rubber products, which accounts for 16 per cent of the cases. Textiles and textile products, base metals and machineries constitute 12, 10 and 8 per cent respectively. It seems that the government policies ultimately benefit a handful of players at the cost of downstream industries and consumer welfare. Injury and definition to the domestic industry is to be re-defined in favour of consumer interests rather than corporate interests. Also, India is taking an average period of 390 days for carrying out the investigations and imposing final duties, which is a long period when compared to other Members.

Table 1.3

Victim of Indian Initiations 1995-2004 (Top 10)

Sl.No	Country	Number of Initiations
1	China P.R	76
2	EU	35
3	Chinese Taipei	29
4	Korea Rep.	28
5	US	21
6	Japan	20
7	Singapore	18
8	Thailand	16
9	Indonesia	15
10	Russia	14

Source: www.wto.org

As seen from Table 1.3, China is the major victim of anti-dumping initiations, which constitute nearly 20 per cent of Indian initiations. Nine and seven per cent of the cases are filed against EU and Taiwan respectively, followed by Korea (7%), US (5%), Japan (5%). It is surprising to note that India initiated 16 anti-dumping cases against Thailand, while the two countries were actively negotiating for a free trade area. Recently, EU brought up a case concerning initiation against a number of product categories to the DSB against India. Taiwan and Bangladesh have also moved DSB against India. Anti-dumping cases always involve huge costs and India as a developing country may not be able to afford defending all these cases in WTO. China is also actively considering taking the cases to WTO. So far,

Russia is not a WTO member and it may not be able to take up the matter to the DSB. However, the burgeoning number of litigations in the DSB may need a lot of manpower and money, which will put tremendous pressure on Indian authorities. Instead of paying huge amount for hiring foreign lawyers, India should develop its own trained manpower in the country to defend its interests in WTO.

Anti-Dumping Initiations Against India

India is also facing a number of initiations from other members of WTO. Since 1995, India faced 105 initiations till December 2004. EU initiated the highest number of cases (26), followed by the US (18), South Africa (17), Indonesia (11), Turkey (6), Canada (5), Argentina and Australia (4 each), Korea and Brazil (3 each), Thailand, Trinidad and Tobago, Egypt and China (2 each). Malaysia, Peru and Poland contributed 1 each.

India has initiated 76 investigations against China, while they initiated only 2 cases against India. During the same period, China had to face 411 initiations by other Members. However, China initiated only 99 investigations against all Members. This shows that there is no evidence of retaliation against those countries who are initiating anti-dumping cases against China. Four countries, namely - the EU, the US, South Africa and Indonesia jointly initiated about 69 per cent of the cases against India.

Figure 1.3

Anti-Dumping Initiations Against India 1995-2004 (Country-wise)

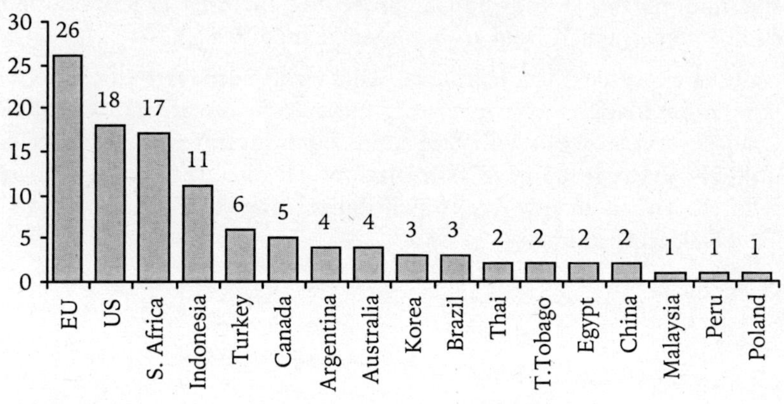

Source: www.wto.org

Conclusion

Michel J. Finger criticises the anti-dumping law as, "the fox put in charge of the hen house: trade restrictions certified by GATT. The fox is clever enough not only to eat the hens, but also to convince the farmer that is the way things ought to be." The supporters of anti-dumping investigations believe that it is for the benefit of the domestic industry. However, economists are finding it difficult to justify any economic benefit or rationale behind imposing anti-dumping duties. Consumer organisations criticise it on the ground that it deprives the consumers from benefits, such as choice of products and cost benefits.

Various methodologies such as "zeroing" and "arms' length" in calculating dumping margin are questionable in nature and helps the developed countries in finding dumping. However, the recent trend that developing countries like India, South Africa and Indonesia have become pioneers in this field and most of the initiations are made against developing countries, is quite alarming.

In India, the trend is very clear and petrochemical imports are always under threat from imposing anti-dumping duties. It is not the duty of the government to protect the monopolies in the country; rather it should concentrate more on the welfare of Small Scale Industries (SSIs), which are affected more by the imposition of anti-dumping duties on imports. They are forced to purchase raw materials from the local monopolies for a higher price than the same in the international market. The ongoing WTO cases will act as a deterrent against India for initiating more investigations in future. Furthermore, the administrative and judicial procedure in India is lengthy and cumbersome, which need to be urgently modified.

It is expected that, in future, China will surpass India in anti-dumping initiations as a retaliatory measure, while at the same time Chinese textile goods will face more dumping investigations. It is unlikely that the number of initiations all over the world will be reduced. This is mainly due to political reasons in developed, as well as, developing countries.

Annex 1

Anti-Dumping Initiations: By Reporting Member
(From: 01-01-95 to 31-12-2004)

Reporting Member	1995	1996	1997	1998	1999	2000	2001	2002	2003	2004	Totals
Argentina	27	22	14	8	23	45	26	14	1	12	192
Australia	5	17	42	13	24	15	23	16	8	9	172
Brazil	5	18	11	18	16	11	17	8	4	8	116
Bulgaria	0	0	0	0	0	0	0	1	0	0	1
Canada	11	5	14	8	18	21	25	5	15	11	133
Chile	4	3	0	2	0	5	0	0	0	0	14
China, P.R.	0	0	0	0	0	6	14	30	22	27	99
Chinese Taipei	0	0	0	0	0	3	3	0	2	0	8
Colombia	4	1	1	6	2	3	6	0	0	0	23
Costa Rica	0	4	1	1	0	0	0	0	0	0	6
Czech Republic	0	0	0	2	1	0	0	0	0	0	3
Ecuador	0	0	0	1	0	0	0	0	0	0	1
Egypt	0	0	7	14	5	1	7	3	1	0	38
European Community	33	25	41	22	65	32	28	20	7	30	303
Guatemala	0	1	0	0	0	0	0	0	0	0	1
India	6	21	13	27	65	41	79	81	46	21	400
Indonesia	0	11	5	8	8	3	4	4	13	4	60
Israel	5	6	3	7	0	1	4	0	0	1	27
Jamaica	0	0	0	0	0	1	1	1	1	0	4
Japan	0	0	0	0	0	0	2	0	0	0	2
Korea, Rep. of	4	13	15	3	6	2	4	9	18	3	77
Latvia	0	0	0	0	0	0	1	6	0	0	7
Lithuania	0	0	0	0	1	6	0	0	0	0	7
Malaysia	3	2	8	1	2	0	1	5	6	3	31
Mexico	4	4	6	12	11	7	5	10	14	6	79
New Zealand	10	4	5	1	4	10	1	2	5	5	47
Nicaragua	0	0	0	2	0	0	0	0	0	0	2
Pakistan	0	0	0	0	0	0	0	0	3	3	6
Panama	0	0	0	2	0	0	0	0	0	0	2
Paraguay	0	0	0	0	1	0	0	0	0	0	1
Peru	2	7	2	3	8	1	8	12	5	7	55
Philippines	1	1	2	3	6	2	0	1	1	0	17
Poland	0	0	1	0	7	0	0	3	1	0	12
Slovenia	0	0	0	0	1	0	0	0	0	0	1
South Africa	16	33	23	41	16	21	6	4	8	5	173

Contd..

...Annex 1 Contd..

Reporting Member	1995	1996	1997	1998	1999	2000	2001	2002	2003	2004	Totals
Thailand	0	1	3	0	0	0	3	21	3	3	34
Trinidad and Tobago	0	1	0	4	3	1	1	0	2	0	12
Turkey	0	0	4	1	8	7	15	18	11	25	89
United States	14	22	15	36	47	47	75	35	37	26	354
Uruguay	0	0	1	0	0	1	4	0	0	0	6
Venezuela	3	2	6	10	7	1	1	1	0	0	31
Totals for 01-01-95 – 31-12-04	157	224	243	256	355	294	364	310	234	209	2646

Source: www.wto.org

2

The Rhetoric and Reality
of U.S. Anti-Dumping Law

BRINK LINDSEY AND DANIEL IKENSON

Introduction

Anti-Dumping laws allow national governments to impose special duties on "unfairly traded" imports. Before duties are imposed, the authorities that administer the law must make two findings: (1) that imported goods are being "dumped," or sold at prices less than "normal value," and (2) that the dumped imports are causing or threatening material injury to the domestic import-competing industry. Under the U.S. system, the Department of Commerce determines whether dumping is occurring, while the International Trade Commission examines whether dumped imports are injuring the domestic industry. When both the DOC and the ITC make affirmative findings, the goods under investigation are subject to duties equal to the margin of dumping—that is, the difference between the U.S. prices of the imports and their "normal value."

Supporters of anti-dumping laws argue that they are needed to create a "level playing field" for domestic industries that face unfair import competition. Specifically, they contend that various distortions in foreign markets—trade barriers, monopoly or collusion, government subsidies, and "barriers to exit" (e.g., poor bankruptcy laws, ineffective protection of creditors' rights) that prevent loss-making businesses from reducing capacity or going out of business—allow foreign producers to charge lower prices in export markets than would otherwise be possible. In one scenario, firms may enjoy supernormal profits at home (in a protected or cartelised "sanctuary market") and then use those profits to cross-subsidise low-price export sales. Alternatively, subsidies or barriers to exit may allow firms to sell abroad (and at home as well) at below-cost prices without suffering the normal marketplace consequences.

According to supporters, anti-dumping laws ensure a level playing field by offsetting artificial sources of competitive advantage. Dumping, it is alleged, demonstrates the existence of one or more of the market distortions discussed above; anti-dumping duties, by making up the difference between dumped prices and "normal value," extinguish the foreign producer's artificial advantage and put the domestic industry back on an equal footing. At least that is the theory.

There is, however, a yawning gap between theory and practice. Anti-dumping laws, contrary to the claims of their supporters, do not ensure a level playing field. Instead, they penalise foreign producers for engaging in commercial practices that are perfectly legal and unexceptionable when engaged in by domestic companies. Such discrimination against foreign firms creates an unlevel playing field for imports. In other words, anti-dumping laws discriminate against imports, and that is the essence of protectionism.

Unfortunately, this particular form of protectionism enjoys the sanction of multilateral trading rules. Article VI of the original General Agreement on Tariffs and Trade authorises national governments to impose duties on dumped imports. Today, the authority to engage in anti-dumping protectionism is recognised by the World Trade Organisation. The WTO Anti-Dumping Agreement, finalised in 1994 during the Uruguay Round of trade talks, specifies the standards and procedures that national anti-dumping regulations must follow. Although, the requirements of this agreement do impose modest restraint on what WTO members can do in the name of anti-dumping, the sad fact is that the agreement allows wide scope for protectionist abuses.

In recent years, many countries have been urging the U.S. government to agree to new international rules at the World Trade Organisation that would tighten the requirements that must be met before anti-dumping protection can be granted. But powerful U.S. lobbying interests, and their supporters in Congress, have vehemently opposed such changes in anti-dumping rules. American industries that frequently seek anti-dumping protection argue that a "strong" law is needed to ensure a level playing field and to maintain public support for generally open markets. They insist that any effort to "weaken" current law through trade negotiations must be rejected out of hand. Unfortunately, there is broad political support for this perspective from Republicans and Democrats alike.

What accounts for this enduring, bipartisan popularity? In the first place, the law's rhetoric is compelling. After all, which members of Congress would like to stand up and say they favour illegal and unfair dumped imports? Who could be opposed to a level playing field? Meanwhile, the reality behind the rhetoric is obscure. The anti-dumping law is notoriously complicated, and its inner workings are known only to a select handful of users, targets, bureaucrats, and lawyers. As a result, most supporters of the law simply take its appealing rhetoric at face value. If it sounds good, it must be good.

Advocates of the U.S. anti-dumping law claim that dumping is an unfair trade practice that takes two different forms: price discrimination and below-cost sales. Both types of dumping allegedly reflect underlying market distortions caused by foreign government policies. Those distortions confer an artificial advantage on foreign producers when they are selling in the United States—they can sell at lower prices than would otherwise be possible.

Thus, price discrimination (i.e., selling at lower prices in the export market than at home) supposedly signals the existence of a protected "sanctuary" home market. According to Greg Mastel, one of the few economists who firmly support the use of anti-dumping laws:

> "If a company engages in dumping in foreign markets and its home market is open, the price differential will induce the company's competitors or other resellers to re-export dumped products to the dumper's home market. These re-exports would quickly pull the home market price down to the dumped price and erase home market profits. Thus, a closed or restricted home market is also a virtual precondition to a successful dumping strategy."

This situation gives the foreign producer an arguably unfair competitive advantage over U.S. rivals. "A closed home market allows companies to charge high prices at home because they face no foreign competition," Mastel explains. "Foreign companies can then use the profits from these domestic sales to cross-subsidise export sales at dumped prices."

As to sales below cost, the contention is that the foreign producer could not sustain its losses in the absence of market-distorting government policies back home. Here again, a domestic sanctuary market could be the culprit: profits at home could allow a company to take losses abroad. Alternatively, government subsidies could prop up a company in spite of its losses. The subsidies might take the form of explicit grants or soft loans, or they might be considerably more subtle.

But does anti-dumping practice match its rhetoric? Are anti-dumping duties, for better or worse, really offsetting the effects of market-distorting government policies? These questions need to be answered in two stages. First, it is necessary to determine the effectiveness of current anti-dumping methodologies at targeting the supposedly unfair pricing practices of price discrimination and selling below cost. Second, to the extent that the anti-dumping law does indeed find its targets, it must be ascertained whether those pricing practices are reliable indicators of underlying market distortions.

Missing the Target

The first step in this inquiry is to review in broad brush how dumping is actually calculated under U.S. law. In general, the DOC compares the prices of imported merchandise sold in the United States to some measure of "normal value." There are, however, a number of different ways to perform such comparisons —and in particular, a number of different benchmarks for determining normal value.

In the most familiar method, the DOC compares "net" U.S. prices to "net" home-market prices. To arrive at net values, the DOC subtracts freight charges, brokerage and handling fees, commissions, and various other selling expenses; the idea here is to compare prices on an "ex-factory" basis.

The anti-dumping statute indicates that comparing U.S. and home-market prices is the preferred method of calculating dumping margins. If specified conditions exist, though, the DOC will employ alternative methodologies. Thus, if the foreign producer does not sell the subject merchandise in the domestic market, or its total domestic sales are less than 5 per cent of its U.S. sales, the home market is considered not viable. In that case the DOC will select another export market to serve as the comparison market; U.S. prices are then compared to prices in some third-country market. If there are no viable third-country markets, the DOC will compare U.S. prices to "constructed value"—which is equal to the company's total cost of production plus some amount for profit.

The DOC can deviate from normal price-to-price comparisons even when there is a viable domestic or third-country market. Within the broad category of merchandise under investigation, there may be many different specific product types or models. For each model sold in the United States, the DOC tries to identify sales of identical or similar products in the comparison market; if it cannot find any such sales, the U.S. sales of that model will be compared to constructed value.

More important, the DOC examines comparison-market prices to determine whether they are below the full cost of production. If more than 20 per cent of comparison-market prices of a particular model are below cost, the DOC will exclude all the below-cost sales of that model from its calculations on the ground that they are "outside the ordinary course of trade." In that case, U.S. prices are compared to above-cost comparison-market prices only; if there are no above-cost sales of identical or similar merchandise, U.S. prices are compared to constructed value.

The DOC employs another methodology altogether for imports from "non-market economies" (NMEs), that is, China, Vietnam, and a few members of the former Soviet bloc. In NME cases, DOC rejects prices as unreliable, since they are not the product of genuine market transactions. Constructed value is also rejected on the ground that the company's costs are likewise not market based. Instead, the DOC obtains the company's "factors of production"—the physical quantities of all the inputs used in producing the merchandise—and values those inputs on the basis of prices in a "surrogate country." Surrogate countries are market economies judged to be at a level of economic development similar to that of the NME country in question. The DOC then compares U.S. prices to a cost-based normal value derived from company-specific factors of production and surrogate-country prices of those factors (including surrogate-country averages for selling, general, and administrative expenses and profit).

Finally, the DOC sometimes calculates dumping on the basis of "facts available" rather than actual company data. Determinations are based on facts available when a foreign producer fails to provide all the price and cost information requested by the DOC, or when the information provided is judged to be inaccurate or incomplete (an ever-present possibility given the byzantine complexity of documentation that foreign companies are required to provide). In those situations, the facts available used by the DOC are generally derived from the allegations contained in the domestic industry's anti-dumping petition.

What do the various calculation methodologies have to do with finding either price discrimination or sales below cost? As it turns out, not very much. As to price discrimination, only one methodology even attempts to measure relevant international price differences; and none of the methodologies seeks to determine whether sales below cost are occurring.

Of all the different ways that the DOC measures dumping, only the straightforward comparison of home-market and U.S. prices is capable of identifying price discrimination that reflects a protected sanctuary market. On the other hand, the apparent price discrimination may be nothing more than an artefact of imperfect price comparisons.

Flawed Methodologies

In the typical anti-dumping investigation, the DOC compares home-market and U.S. prices of physically different goods, in different kinds of packaging, sold at different times, in different and fluctuating currencies, to different customers at different levels of trade, in different quantities, with different freight and other movement costs, different credit terms, and other differences in directly associated selling expenses (e.g., commissions, warranties, royalties, and advertising). Is it any wonder that the prices are not identical?

Admittedly, the DOC's dumping calculation methodologies try to adjust for some of the differences, but the adjustments are necessarily imprecise. For example, when the DOC compares physically different merchandise, it adjusts for differences in materials, direct labour, and variable overhead costs. While this makes a certain amount of sense, in a real-world commercial context it goes without saying that actual price differences may be more or less than the differences in variable manufacturing costs. And in many cases, the DOC makes no adjustment. Thus, prices of goods sold in the United States may be compared to prices of goods sold many months earlier or later in the home-market without any adjustment for market fluctuations over the intervening time. And although, unit prices typically decline with larger order quantities, the DOC rarely adjusts for quantity discounts.

Critics of anti-dumping have focused considerable attention on asymmetries in the DOC's methodologies that produce a bias in favour of finding price differences. Without a doubt, such asymmetries exist. But the more fundamental and too often neglected problem is that the practice of comparing each and every U.S. sale to some sale in the home-market will produce spurious price differences that are purely the product of "apples-and-oranges" comparisons.

Whatever the problems associated with comparing home-market and U.S. prices, at least such comparisons bear directly on the question of international price discrimination and possible sanctuary markets. By contrast, the other methodologies have nothing to do with finding relevant international price differences.

Thus, a comparison of U.S. and third-country prices can possibly show international price discrimination, but it cannot reveal a sanctuary market. Any foreign producer under investigation is an "outsider" as far as all third-country market is concerned; it is hindered, not helped, by any government barriers that block access to its export sales. If for some reason the company is earning higher prices in that third-country, the reason clearly is not that government-imposed barriers are shielding it from competition. On the contrary, it had to overcome any barriers that were present in that third-country market to be selling there at all. Meanwhile, prices charged in a third-country indicate nothing about whether a firm's home-market is closed.

Comparison of U.S. prices to a cost-based normal value—whether it is derived from the company's own costs (in constructed-value cases) or from surrogate-country prices (in NME cases)—cannot show price discrimination, for the simple reason that price data are not used for one side of the comparison. Furthermore, a finding of dumping using constructed value offers no evidence of the existence of a sanctuary home-market. All such a finding can show is that *U.S. sales* are being made *below* some baseline level of profitability; it cannot show that *home-market sales* are *above* any similar baseline, since home-market sales are excluded from the dumping calculation.

Indeed, when constructed value is used because there are no above-cost sales of identical or similar merchandise in the home market, the available evidence weighs *against* the existence of a sanctuary market. A sanctuary market is one in which a foreign company is making profits due to government intervention; here, though, the company is apparently losing money at home. The supposed source of unfair advantage—namely, the opportunity to cross-subsidise low-price export sales—is missing.

The situation is similar when U.S. sales are compared to above-cost sales only. A dumping finding based on such comparisons tells us nothing about the existence of international price discrimination, since the comparisons are skewed: low-price sales have been excluded from the home-market side, but not the U.S. side. And here again, as in constructed-value cases, the evidence affirmatively rebuts claims of a sanctuary market. Below-cost sales are excluded only when they constitute at least 20 per cent of sales; such widespread losses are inconsistent with the supposedly supernormal profits of a sanctuary market.

Finally, a dumping finding based on facts available provides no evidence of either price discrimination or a sanctuary market. The facts available are generally taken from the domestic industry's anti-dumping petition, hardly a source of objective analysis. Indeed, it is expressly recognised that determinations on the basis of facts available are punitive; it is the threat of such determinations that is used to compel foreign producers' cooperation with the DOC's often onerous information requests. In any event, the dumping allegations in anti-dumping petitions are often based on estimates of constructed value, and thus are incapable of substantiating the existence of price discrimination or a sanctuary market.

If the anti-dumping law takes poor aim at price discrimination, it fires completely blindly when it comes to sales below cost. Not one of the methodologies employed by the DOC measures whether imported merchandise is sold at a loss. The DOC does determine whether home-market or third-country sales are below cost in deciding whether to exclude them as "outside the ordinary course of trade." That inquiry, though, is irrelevant to the issue of whether *U.S. sales* are below cost.

The closest the DOC comes to determining whether U.S. sales are made at a loss is in constructed-value and NME cases. In those cases, the DOC does calculate the production costs of the merchandise sold in the United States, but then it adds an amount for profit before the resulting normal value is compared to U.S. sales prices. Thus, the criterion for deciding whether imports are unfairly traded under this methodology is, not the existence of losses, but insufficient profitability. Sales at a loss are considered dumped, but so are profitable sales if the profit rate is too low.

That over-inclusiveness is exacerbated by the specific way in which dumping margins are calculated in cost-based cases. The DOC compares average U.S. prices of specific models to a single product-wide or industry-wide profitability rate. Sales below the profitability benchmark are considered dumped; sales above the benchmark are deemed to have dumping margins of zero. Consequently, even if U.S. sales average a "normal" profit, dumping will be found simply because profit rates vary by model.

Finally, there is an additional layer of methodological distortion in NME cases. In those cases, the cost data used are not those of the firm under investigation; instead, surrogate values from another country are applied to that firm's factors of production. This methodology is fraught with potential for gross inaccuracy. The extent to which the end-result bears any relation to market-based costs is open to serious question.

Examining the Case Record

To evaluate the problems with current anti-dumping practice in fuller detail, we examined all DOC final determinations through December 31, 1998, in original anti-dumping investigations initiated since January 1, 1995. This sample includes 141 company-specific dumping determinations in 49 different anti-dumping investigations. The DOC made affirmative dumping findings for 107 of the 141 companies investigated and in 48 of the 49 investigations. The average dumping margin in the sample, including all the zero and *de minimis* dumping findings, is 44.68 per cent.

The most striking fact that emerges from a review of this case record is how few anti-dumping determinations have anything to do with targeting—or even attempting to target—price discrimination associated with possible sanctuary markets. Price discrimination bulks very large in anti-dumping rhetoric but commands much less attention in actual anti-dumping practice.

Of the 141 total determinations, 36 were based on facts available rather than actual company data. Another 47 of the determinations are from the 14 NME investigations included in the sample. In 16 of the determinations, constructed value was used either because there was no viable comparison market or because there were no identical or similar products sold in the comparison market. For 37 determinations, at least 20 per cent of the sales of some or all comparison products were below cost, so the DOC compared U.S. prices to some combination of comparison-market prices, above-cost comparison-market prices only, and constructed value. And one determination was based purely on a comparison of U.S. and third-country prices.

That leaves only 4 determinations in which the DOC calculated dumping strictly on the basis of comparisons of U.S. and home-market prices. Furthermore, in 2 of the 4 determinations in question, the DOC concluded that there was zero or *de minimis* dumping. Thus, in only 2 of the 107 total affirmative determinations (both of which were made in the same investigation) did the DOC find dumping by relying exclusively on the currently used calculation methodology that bears any *possible* connection to the existence of market-distorted price discrimination.

Another 31 determinations, encompassing 17 different investigations, relied partially on comparisons of U.S. and home-market prices. In all of those determinations, however, the DOC skewed at least some of the comparisons by using only above-cost home-market sales, or by substituting constructed value for actual price data. In those mixed cases, the DOC found dumping in 25 of the determinations. For those determinations, however, it is impossible to tell from the public record how much of each dumping margin is attributable to normal comparisons of U.S. and home-market prices, how much to comparisons of U.S. prices and above-cost prices only, and how much to comparisons of U.S. prices and constructed value. In other words, there is insufficient publicly available information to distinguish between the "signal" of international price differences and the "noise" of dumping margins generated by methodologies that do not detect price differences.

There are good grounds for assuming that the "noise" is considerable. Mixing methodologies tends to increase dumping margins above what would be found if only normal price-to-price comparisons were made. Comparing U.S. sales to only above-cost sales always exaggerates dumping margins, since all the lowest-price sales are excluded from the comparison. And resort to constructed value often exaggerates dumping margins because of the artificially high profit rates that are frequently used.

In sum, a review of the actual case record confirms that the anti-dumping law as currently written and implemented is miserably ineffective at identifying price discrimination caused by sanctuary markets. In only 27 of the 107 affirmative determinations, or 25.2 per cent of that total, did the DOC make at least some use of the only methodology relevant to detecting price discrimination, and all but 2 of those determinations were distorted by resort to other methodologies. Meanwhile, in the other 80 affirmative determinations, or 74.8 per cent of the total, there is absolutely nothing in the DOC's findings that in any way points to the existence of price discrimination.

What about the anti-dumping law's track record with respect to the other form of dumping—below-cost sales caused by market distortions? In as many as 100 of the 141 determinations in the sample, the DOC relied fully or partially on cost-based analysis. Nearly half of the determinations—67 of 141—depend exclusively on comparisons of U.S. prices to some cost-based benchmark of normal value. In 20 of those cases, the DOC used the foreign producer's own cost information to calculate constructed value; the remaining 47 were NME cases in which the DOC calculated costs using surrogate-country values. In an additional 33 determinations, the DOC made at least some use of constructed value in its calculations, although perhaps not in every determination.

The most obvious problem with all of the cost-based determinations is that they do not attempt to measure whether U.S. sales are below cost. As discussed above, they measure instead whether U.S. sales are below some measure of cost plus profit. Because of the inclusion of profit, sales can be considered dumped even when they are above cost, and the dumping margins of below-cost sales are exaggerated.

Market Distortions Assumed, Not Proven

The evidence reviewed shows that the anti-dumping law is highly prone to finding dumping even when there is no price discrimination or selling below cost. But there is another, deeper problem with the law. Namely, it simply assumes that those pricing practices, when found, indicate the existence of government-caused market distortions. As shown below, this assumption is entirely unwarranted.

It is true that international price differences can reveal a sanctuary home-market. Likewise, sales below cost, under certain circumstances, can signal the presence of government-caused market distortions. But just the fact that they *can* does not mean that they usually *do*. There are many other possible explanations—explanations that rest entirely on normal business practices and have nothing to do with any "unfair" competitive advantage. By assuming that margins of dumping can only reflect foreign market distortions and, thus, ignoring alternative causes of the pricing behavior it targets, the anti-dumping law routinely punishes foreign firms for normal commercial conduct.

Price Differences and Sanctuary Markets

The lack of connection between affirmative dumping determinations and evidence of sanctuary markets is not surprising. The methodological flaws in pure price-to-price comparisons, compounded by the practice of using both price-to-price and cost-based comparisons in a single case, can result in findings of dumping even when there is no real pattern of international price differences. Furthermore, even when anti-dumping investigations do stumble onto cases of actual price discrimination, they are incapable of distinguishing between those that reflect the existence of a sanctuary market and those that are attributable to normal commercial factors. There are in fact many unexceptionable business reasons for charging more in one market than in another, and the persistence of those price differences over time by no means proves that the high-price market is closed.

International price differences can arise when a firm's status differs between national markets. A consumer goods firm may enjoy brand recognition in its home-market that allows it to command a premium price; while abroad its brand name may be less valuable. Similarly, a producer goods firm may have built a reputation at home as a reliable supplier of high-quality products, while remaining relative unknown one in foreign markets. Or it may have carefully cultivated long-term business relationships with its domestic customers, while serving export markets on more of a spot-market basis. In all of those situations, the firm is exposed to greater pricing pressure abroad than at home and consequently will be forced to accept a lower price on its export sales.

Price differences can also result when the market structures or conditions in which a firm must operate vary from country to country. For example, market concentration may be higher in the firm's home-market than abroad, and pricing pressures may consequently be less severe. Or numerical market concentration may have nothing to do with it; the vagaries of business culture and market history may combine to render a firm's home market less prone to aggressive price-cutting than a particular export market.

The resulting price differences across national markets in these examples reflect purely commercial factors and have nothing to do with government intervention or sanctuary markets.

Sales Below Cost and Market Distortions

Just as price discrimination can reflect the existence of market distortions, so can below-cost pricing be associated with "abnormal" market behaviour. First, sales below *marginal* cost generally do not make commercial sense. While sales above marginal cost (but below full unit cost) at least make some contribution to recovering sunk costs, sales below marginal cost only compound total losses and, therefore, are almost always to be avoided. Likewise, firms cannot normally sell below full unit costs for a protracted period of time. Over the long term, chronic loss-making firms cannot attract the capital needed to stay in business. In these scenarios, firms exhibiting a pattern of making losses—whether of the acute, marginal cost variety or the chronic, below-unit-cost variety—may be benefiting from some form of government intervention that allows them to ignore normal market signals.

The usual reason for sales at a loss is nothing other than a normal, healthy, competitive marketplace. In the United States, for example, of the 4.47 million U.S. corporations that filed tax returns in 1995, only 2.46 million—or 55 per cent—reported any net income. Even the mightiest corporations are not immune from red ink. Looking back a few years, General Motors lost money three years in a row during 1990-92, with accumulated pre-tax losses of $11.4 billion in that period. IBM posted two straight years of negative earnings in 1992 and 1993, racking up a staggering $17.8 billion of pre-tax losses—14 cents in the red for every dollar of sales.

Sales at a loss can indicate all kinds of normal market phenomena. Companies that are going out of business generally leave a trail of red ink on the way out. Other times, losses are only temporary, as companies make mistakes or business conditions deteriorate; companies can get back in the black by correcting errors and riding out the storm. During down periods, it may make good business sense to go on producing at a loss instead of cutting back production. For example, there may be long-term strategic benefits that accompany a certain market position (and market share); staying the market leader through a temporary downturn may maximise long-term profitability.

Also, if a downturn is seen as too temporary to justify permanent capacity cutbacks, it may pay to continue producing instead of allowing capacity to go idle. Here the distinction between marginal and sunk costs, or their real-world equivalents of variable and fixed costs, is crucial. If a company can continue to produce and sell goods above variable costs, it can at least make some contribution to fixed costs—costs that would be incurred even if those goods had not been produced. Under these conditions—which are typical for industries that face cyclical peaks and troughs of demand—continuing to produce and sell minimises total losses during the downturn.

For young companies, losses are not just common; they are the norm. Investment must come first, followed (eventually, if all goes well) by returns on that investment. In these circumstances, even fast-growing companies can generate significant red ink. Meanwhile, for established companies, losses are common on new products. By virtue of the well-known phenomenon of the "learning curve," production costs tend to decline in line with cumulative production volume. Knowing this, businesses often price new goods below full current cost in order to increase sales volumes and accelerate passage down the learning curve. Such a strategy is intended to maximise profitability over the full life cycle of the product.

Eventually, of course, companies must turn a profit on their overall operations if they are to stay in business. Likewise, specific products must generally earn a profit sooner or later or else be dropped from a company's business line. There are, however, important exceptions. On some products, companies can lose money indefinitely; indeed, under certain conditions they may be well advised to do so.

For example, a multi-product firm may intentionally charge a money-losing price for one good to encourage higher sales of another good. Such a "cross-subsidisation" strategy, if successful, can actually maximise overall firm profits.

Selling below full unit costs may also make sense in the case of so-called co-products or joint products—two or more different goods that are produced simultaneously in the same manufacturing process. Examples include different cuts of meat from the same animal, different ores extracted in the same mining operation, different chemicals produced by the same reaction, and products of varying quality produced in the same manufacturing batch. For those types of products, some allocation of shared manufacturing costs among the various joint products is necessary for cost-accounting purposes. Depending on how costs are allocated, a given co-product may show a profit or a loss.

In sum, sales below cost can mean many things other than the presence of government-caused market distortions. The anti-dumping law, however, completely ignores this possibility. When below-cost sales do end up getting caught in the wide net thrown in constructed-value and NME cases, the DOC's calculation methodologies fail to distinguish between normal commercial losses and those that point to the existence of government interventionism. As a result, anti-dumping law too often penalises normal commercial practices having nothing to do with anyone's definition of unfair trade.

For the existence of below-cost sales to raise any serious question of government interventionism, the losses must either be acute (i.e., sales must be below variable costs) or chronic (i.e., losses must persist for a period of years).

For chronic losses, the period investigated by the DOC in anti-dumping cases is only 12 months. Consequently, the DOC lacks the evidentiary record to determine whether a company's losses are abnormally persistent. Because the DOC does not take a longer view, it cannot determine whether losses reflect a temporary market downturn or business reversal, or whether they flow from a conscious growth-oriented strategy for a new company or a new product. Likewise, anti-dumping investigations develop no evidentiary record for determining whether acute or chronic losses, to the extent they exist, have a reasonable commercial explanation.

Most fundamental, the DOC does not examine whether the supposedly below-cost U.S. sales it identifies are in any way connected with government interventionism in the home market. There is no investigation of whether trade barriers or other restrictions on competition create a domestic sanctuary market that bankrolls losses abroad; nor of whether the foreign producer receives government grants, soft loans, special tax breaks, preferential access to credit on non-commercial terms, or any other form of assistance that supports its loss-making operations; nor of whether there are basic structural flaws in a country's economic policy that impede normal market responses to losses.

Conclusion

The anti-dumping law is defended as a remedy for market distortions caused by foreign government policies. Yet in actual practice, the methods of determining dumping under the law fail, repeatedly and at multiple levels, to distinguish between normal commercial pricing practices and those that reflect market-distorting government policies.

As a result, the anti-dumping law as it currently exists routinely punishes normal competitive business practices—practices commonly engaged in by American companies at home and abroad. It is, therefore, not the case that the law guarantees a level playing field for American companies and their foreign competitors. On the contrary, it actively discriminates against foreign goods by subjecting them to requirements not applicable to American products.

An anti-dumping law that actually did target government-caused market distortions would look very different from the law in its present form. Bringing the reality of anti-dumping practice into line with the rhetoric of anti-dumping supporters would require dramatic reforms. Such reform faces formidable obstacles. Use of anti-dumping laws around the world is widespread and growing; and wherever those laws operate, the protectionist status quo enjoys the support of entrenched bureaucracies and import-competing corporate interests. In the United States in particular, energetic and well-organised protectionist lobbies have mobilised nearly overwhelming political support for their position on anti-dumping issues. As a result, for many years the world's most powerful country and leader of the multilateral trading system has stood as the principal opponent of meaningful changes in anti-dumping rules.

Of all the obstacles hindering anti-dumping reforms, however, none is greater than ignorance. Failure to understand how anti-dumping laws actually operate in practice—and how they fail so spectacularly to do what their supporters say they are supposed to do—lies at the root of much of the resistance to anti-dumping reform. Many supporters of the anti-dumping status quo honestly believe that these laws in their present form are necessary to combat unfair trading practices and thereby ensure a level playing field. If those supporters fully understood the reality of contemporary anti-dumping practice—if they understood how frequently trade-restrictive measures are inflicted on normal, healthy competition—their opposition to needed reforms would likely to soften.

Of course, protectionist interests support the anti-dumping status quo so fervently precisely because of its flaws. Their goal is to squelch foreign competition in whatever way they can, and the anti-dumping law in its current form has proved very handy indeed. And because of ignorance about the law's complex workings, protectionist interests are able to cloak their special pleading in the high-minded rhetoric of fairness and concern for a level playing field. If they were forced to defend the status quo honestly, for the protectionist scam that it is, they would find it much harder to win adherents to their cause. Accordingly, education and clarification should be the top priorities of those advocating anti-dumping reform.

3

Anti-Dumping in the European Union

FREDRIK ERIXON

Introduction

Trade policy moves in mysterious ways. Since the late-eighteenth century, indeed perhaps even longer, there have been ample of evidence of the economic and political benefits of free trade. Equally, the evidence of the failures of trade protectionism has been at the centre stage of the policy debate for the same period. Yet countries and politicians have time and again succumbed to protectionism. As Ulysses in the great Homer classic, politicians have listened to the fatal siren calls of protectionism, although being in full knowledge of that free trade and international economic integration is a superior choice.

The noble idea of unilateral free trade, the governing principle of the international economy in the late-nineteenth century, was punctuated in the mid-war period. The attempt to restore the pre-1914 order after the First World War had failed bitterly, already in the 1920s, and many countries started to increase the tariff lines and overall developed a *beggar-thy-neighbour* policy poisoning international economic integration. In 1930 the United States introduced the notorious Smooth-Hawley Tariff Act and raised the level of tariff protection from 38 to 52 per cent. A few months' later Australia, Canada, Cuba, France, Italy, Spain, and New Zealand followed suit and before long Great Britain, the home of the tradition of unilateral free trade, put the final nail in the coffin by opting for import protection. Since then, trade policy has largely been governed by a multilateral organisation and by principles bordering to mercantilism. As economist Paul Krugman once described modern trade policy:

"To make sense of international trade negotiations, one needs to remember three simple rules about the objectives of negotiating countries:

1. Exports are good.

2. Imports are bad.

3. Other things equal, an equal increase in import and exports is good.

In other words, GATT-think is enlightened mercantilism."

Following the principle of enlightened mercantilism, the process of trade liberalisation in the post-war period has turned into a game of concessions. The mechanism of reciprocity—'I do what you do'—has enforced the mercantilist notion of trade policy reforms and steered attention away from the true idea of free trade: unilateral trade liberalisation acknowledging that my country will benefit from decreased trade protection regardless of other countries choices. Free trade is primarily about getting access to goods and services that other countries can produce more efficiently. Therefore, trade protections are more damaging for the importing country than for the exporting country.

The latest development in EU-China trade relations is a case in point. In June 2005, the EU and China agreed to introduce a new system of quotas for 10 categories of textile products that are exported from China to the European Union. This followed the ten-year expiry period of the quota system in the WTO Agreement on Textiles and Clothing (ATC) from the Uruguay Round. However, the EU, as well as other countries using trade protection to curb its textile imports, did not prepare for the end of the quota system and soon after the New Year (the quotas expired on January 1, 2005) the EU Commission and the Council of Ministers faced heavy lobbying from the textile-producing interest group, Euratex, arguing for new protection.

The EU Commission responded to their call by forcing China to an agreement curbing Chinese export of 10 categories of textiles to 2008. In all crucial respects, this is a measure similar to an import tariff in the European Union; the purpose and the effect of the export restraint is to lower the export of particular products from China to the EU.

Now, the question is why did all this happen? EU consumers had clearly benefited from the new open trade regime; the cost of clothes had fallen significantly in this short period and was about to fall even further as new Chinese imports reached the market. In Sweden some financial analysts even voiced concerns about the rapidly falling prices of clothing and how that would strengthen general deflationary pressures and cause macroeconomic imbalances.

Fuelled by the rising export, Chinese companies, in their turn, had been able to expand the production of textiles. Despite this so-called win-win situation for China and Europe, the EU Commission pushed heavily for new trade protectionism, claiming that European producers needed more time to adjust to the new competition. Thus, the Commission branded the new protection as an attempt to 'manage change and adjustment rather than manage trade.'

But this is not the full story, only the tip of the iceberg. The EU had started investigations to measure up possible efforts to limit Chinese exports under the Textiles Specific Safeguard Clause in China's WTO Accession Protocol. A process of WTO consultation had also been started. The EU was apparently in search of every accessible method to block rising imports from China. The main purpose was undoubtedly to lower the competition for European textile producers, but the EU also labelled these efforts as an attempt to protect, or rather stimulate, an idea of 'equal trading opportunities' for poor and emerging countries. China, the argument was, is too an efficient producer and 'take' European market shares from other exporting countries that are also poor and in need of export opportunities. Therefore, the EU argued for a development-oriented view on trade policies that promotes export from countries that are not sufficiently competitive.

The Economics of Anti-Dumping

The new system of quotas is not directly an anti-dumping measure, but it is a safeguard and bears close resemblance to the *motif* of many anti-dumping actions initiated by the European Union. One particular resemblance is that this new voluntary export restraint, as most actions taken under the anti-dumping heading, has nothing to do with 'dumping' or 'unfair' trade at all.

There are several categories of 'dumping' actions, procedures, and motivations. Economists generally speak about three types of dumping motivations from an exporting company. First of all there exists a market-expansion dumping that is based on differences in demand between two particular markets. After the Asian financial crisis in 1997-1998, domestic demand in Southeast Asia declined sharply and since China did not devalue its currency, as many other countries in the region did at the time, the price of Chinese export rose sharply and had to be redirected to other markets, in particular to the US and the European Union. This example illustrates aspects of market expansion, but also leads us to another motivation for dumping, cyclical dumping. Cyclical dumping usually occurs when demand fall rapidly or when there is an oversupply of the particular product. Thirdly, economists identify state trading dumping when a non-market economy creates, deliberately or not, an oversupply that subsequently is dumped on a market.

None of these motivations for dumping do generally cause trouble in trade relations. But in combination with other measures, they can result in situations that clearly hinder a free and fair trading order based on the principles of the market economy. Two practices are of particular concern.

A company can sell their products on export markets to very low prices in order to obtain monopoly power by effectively making it impossible for competitors to stay in the market. To proponents of anti-dumping actions, this is allegedly a normal procedure in many markets and distorts not only trade but also economic efficiency in other ways. Once the predatory company has obtained monopoly power it can raise prices and profits. The company is not any longer constrained by normal market competition from other competitors.

This seems to be a situation where consumers clearly stand to loose from unfair trading practices. However, the case for anti-dumping measures to curb the behaviour of predatory companies is not as clear-cut as many assumes.

The sheer presence of a monopoly situation does not necessarily translate into rising prices. A monopolist faces competition from other products that can substitute the monopoly product and as long as there are no legal restrictions to enter a particular market, there is always a possibility of other companies entering the market if the monopoly company raise prices and increase profits. This is, *mutatis mutandis*, the prime explanation to why monopolies in most circumstances are only temporarily and why it is difficult to maintain price hikes. As have been shown by economist William Baumol and others, the presence of free entry and exit in a market tempers the predatory ambitions of monopolists.

To be a successful strategy, predatory dumping moreover requires a few additional prerequisites. The predatory company need a large market share at home that is protected, or in other ways function as a sanctuary market, and must have the possibility to obtain large market shares in another country. In case there are several competing companies in the home-market they must in some way collude if they should be able to keep high prices after the companies in the foreign market have been driven out.

The second concern is similar to the market expansion dumping discussed above but is not primarily about gaining control over a foreign market. Rather it is based on a situation where a company has a protected home-market and compete in an industry with typical economies of scale characteristics. If a company has access to both a home- and a foreign-market it can divide costs between these two locations and, thus, gets a cost advantage over a company from another market that is not able or prohibited to access the first company's home-market. This 'strategic' dumping will sooner or later result in increased market power for the company with a cost advantage and, subsequently, price hikes and lowered economic efficiency.

These two concerns of the effects of dumping is part and parcel of the rhetoric of anti-dumping actions, in the European Union as well as in other countries. However, it is rarely that a government institution or agency provides sufficient evidence to prove that market expansion dumping or strategic dumping really exists and that it lowers the welfare of consumers. Of greater concern to the world trading community is that few countries today, the EU in particular, bothers to investigate in detail whether a particular situation really is based on dumping and if it causes harm to consumers.

Anti-Dumping Policy and Actions in the European Union

The EU rules to tackle dumping dates back to the earliest days of the community. Following the completion of the Uruguay Round, a new set of rules came into force on January 1, 1995 that replaced the old regulation. A few changes were also made in 1996 that are of importance to the procedure of investigating and deciding whether anti-dumping actions are called-for or not.

The Commission is responsible for investigating complaints from parties allegedly harmed by dumping from third country firm and, thus, also responsible for assessing whether the complaints are justified. In addition, the Commission can also impose provisional measures and in some cases also definite measures (if it concerns coal and steel products). However, as a general rule, it is the Council of Ministers that decides upon definite anti-dumping actions. In other words, it is a forum of elected politicians that decides whether anti-dumping duties should be imposed.

The European Community rules for anti-dumping provide for the imposition of anti-dumping duties when the following conditions are met:

i) *A Finding of Dumping*: The export price at which the product is sold on the Community market is shown to be lower than the price on the producer's home-market.

ii) *A Material Injury to Community Industry*: The imports have caused or threaten to cause damage to a substantial segment of the industry within the European Community, such as a loss of market share, reduced prices for producers and resulting pressure on production, sales, profits, productivity, etc.

iii) *The Interest of the Community*: The costs for the Community of taking measures must not be disproportionate to the benefits.

In other words, an industry, a company or a group of companies in the European Union that considers import from a non-EU country to be dumped and causing material injury to the industry, can submit a complaint to the Commission, directly or through its national government. Within 45 days the Commission will then examine the complaint, consult the member states and subsequently decide whether or not there is sufficient evidence to merit a formal investigation. If there is not evidence or, *nota bene*, if the complainants not represent at least 25 per cent of the total EU production in question, the complaint shall be rejected.

A formal investigation normally does not take more than a year. During that time period the Commission may impose provisional duties. These duties cannot exceed the difference between the price on the home-market and the export price on the EU market. Furthermore, they are not allowed to last more than nine months. After nine months, the Council must decide whether the anti-dumping actions should be prolonged. If a third country consider an imposed anti-dumping in the EU to be unfair or not in tune with agreements, they can turn to the WTO dispute settlement mechanism or challenge the anti-dumping action in the European Court of First Instance.

Anti-dumping measures are, as in other WTO member countries, basically governed by the WTO rules in GATT Article VI, and are embodied in various forms. An *ad valorem* duty is a fixed percentage of the CIF prices before payment of customs duty. A *Specific duty* is a fixed amount per unit imported. There is also a duty based on an amount equal to the difference between the price of a product at the European Community frontier and a fixed price established by the EC Commission.

Earlier, price undertakings were a common result of an anti-dumping procedure, in particular between China and the European Union. A price undertaking is a voluntary price hike by the exporter, in other words a voluntary method to restrain exports. The rules for price undertakings in the European Union are not well articulated, leaving a considerable discretion to the EU Commission and the Council of Ministers. However, since the 1990s the EU has been much less inclined to accept offer of price undertakings from foreign companies and instead opted for *ad valorem* duties. Up to 1990 about 30 per cent of all anti-dumping cases ended in a price undertaking, but since then the role of price undertaking has diminished. This is a good development. A legal based trading order should rely on duties rather than voluntary price undertakings. Moreover, duties are more likely to result in so-called 'anti-dumping jumping' – substituting exports with foreign direct investments (FDI), instead of exporting a particular product to the EU a company invest in production facilities in the EU–which subsequently promotes higher price competition within the EU.

Two crucial aspects of the EU anti-dumping procedure need to be highlighted. The first aspect concerns the method of deciding definite anti-dumping measures. Decisions are usually taken (unless it concerns coal and steel products) by the Council of Ministers, which is a forum of elected politicians. The sheer idea, or presence, of an elected body deciding matters concerning compliance of rules is not only surprising but also subject to criticism. It is a practice that is arguably not in tune with democratic ideas and praxis; elected politicians shall decide rules but should not be monitoring or policing them. In addition, such a procedure opens the whole process of anti-dumping impositions to other considerations than the pure economical concerns stated in the Community rules.

It is obvious from a political economy perspective that this method invites political concerns to be taken into consideration;

representatives of a country or a region with companies that could stand to benefit from an anti-dumping duty have a political interest to support an anti-dumping petition whether it is in the general welfare interest of the EU or not. The risk of being faced with heavy opposition from domestic interest groups is often sufficient to close the proceedings for economic rationality. In particular if a decision is close to a parliamentary election, then the general interest is easily suffered on the altar of a local interest in conflict with the public good. Political economy considerations are also strengthened by the lack of voting transparency in the Council. Although, it is often leaked how a particular country has voted in the Council, votes are in principle a secret and not subject to public scrutiny.

In 2004 the voting rules were also changed in a way that leads to a bias in favour of imposing anti-dumping measures. Before the change anti-dumping duties could only be made definite after the Council of Ministers had approved it in a simple majority vote where abstentions counted as a vote against imposing an anti-dumping duty. Since March 2004, however, abstentions count as a vote in favour of imposing an anti-dumping measure. Opposing an anti-dumping action has to be a proactive choice rather than the other way around. In other words, the 'default position' is in favour of protectionism.

The second aspect concerns the evidence in favour of anti-dumping actions. As in the United States, the ground for anti-dumping actions is, besides material injury to EU industry, an observation of a so-called 'dumping margin,' a difference in price between sales on the home market and the export price on EU markets. True, there is also sort of a Community Interest Clause pointing to the need for a general welfare interest in the EU to be present in order to legitimate anti-dumping actions. But that principle is rarely tested and, alas, do generally not govern EU policies.

The methods of calculating the dumping margin can in formal investigations be very complicated and difficult to understand even for experienced analysts of anti-dumping policies. But the major concern here is principally not the merits of various methods of investigating dumping practices; the concern is rather the nature of the definition of dumping. Primarily because a lower price on the EU market than in, say, the Indian market is not an injury to consumers. On the contrary, if a foreign company sell their product at a lower price in the EU than they do at home it is rather beneficial for the EU consumers.

In particular because the export price of a foreign company is lower than the price of the domestic EU producer (anti-dumping actions does not concern foreign companies that sell to higher prices than EU producers in the EU market).

What is more, from the sheer presence of a difference in price between an exporter's home-market and the EU market does not follow a presence of dumping, injury to domestic producers or predatory pricing practices hurting consumers. In fact, a price difference alone does not mean anything of the kind. Price differences are very normal parts of an international economy and often reflect markets differences. If prices were not to reflect market differences, differences in demand as well as differences on the supply side, it would not only be a static loss to consumers but also hamper natural market responses and the dynamic development of the market.

Admittedly, the philosophy of anti-dumping actions is partly intended to be in opposition to basic economics. But the practise of anti-dumping has moved away from its original purposes and is now largely used as a common protectionist measure to stifle competition, whether the competition is unfair or not. A closer look on how the European Union is acting in the realm of anti-dumping will provide ample of evidence of the political economy of anti-dumping actions.

The European Union is, however, not the most notorious user of anti-dumping action. The United States has for many decades been the main perpetrator of the use of anti-dumping measures and continues to be the country with the highest number of anti-dumping measures in place. During 1995-2000, the average number of anti-dumping measures in place was 323 for the United States, followed by the European Union (143), Canada (88), Mexico (84), and South Africa (59). The corresponding figure for the world total was 976.

This definitely testifies a sharp increase in the use of anti-dumping measures. Anti-Dumping cases numbered 2113 between 1990 and 1999, which is an increase about a third from the 1401 cases between 1980 and 1989. Another major trend in the use of anti-dumping measure is the rapid rise of anti-dumping actions taken by developing countries. Formerly a practice mainly employed by developed countries, it is now used by many developing countries as well— Brazil, China, India and South Africa in particular. In only six years (1995-2000), South Africa's share of the number of anti-dumping measures in place rose from 2 per cent to 10 per cent. During the same period, India's share of the world total grew even faster, from 1.5 per cent in 1995 to 9 per cent in 2000.

This development seems set to continue. In 2003-2004, Brazil, China, India and South Africa accounted for 32 per cent of all new initiations of anti-dumping investigations. True, most developing countries have lately followed the global trend of a small but at least observable fall in the number of new anti-dumping investigations and final anti-dumping measures, but developing countries continues to increase their share in the total number of anti-dumping investigations and actions.

There are various explanations to the trend of increased use of anti-dumping actions in the developing world. Part of the explanation is that developing countries have generally gained strength—in world trade policy affairs as well as in their share of the world trade volume—and now reciprocate, or perhaps retaliate, with the same unfriendly measures.

Another explanation takes stock against the trend of trade liberalisations during the last decades; as tariffs have been lowered, quotas expired and developing countries generally opened up their economies to the world, anti-dumping initiations have been one course of action still open for general protectionism. The same is true on the global level: the rise in the number of anti-dumping measures is closely related to the decline in tariff protections.

Put differently, the rise in the number of anti-dumping filings in the developing world seems not to be related to any rise in dumping practises, by firms in developed countries or their counterparts in the developing world.

The EU share of the number of anti-dumping cases has declined with the rise of the developing country share. As shown in Figure 3.1, EU represented in 2003 approximately five per cent of all anti-dumping actions taken. Measured differently, as the share of the total anti-dumping measures in place, the EU represented 14 per cent during the period 1995-2000.

In the last five years, the number of investigations and impositions of definite anti-dumping measures have also declined. As shown in Table 3.1, the number of new investigations in 2004 was a bit higher than the average for the last five years, but as a trend the number of investigations is declining.

Figure 3.1

EU Share of Anti-Dumping Actions (%)

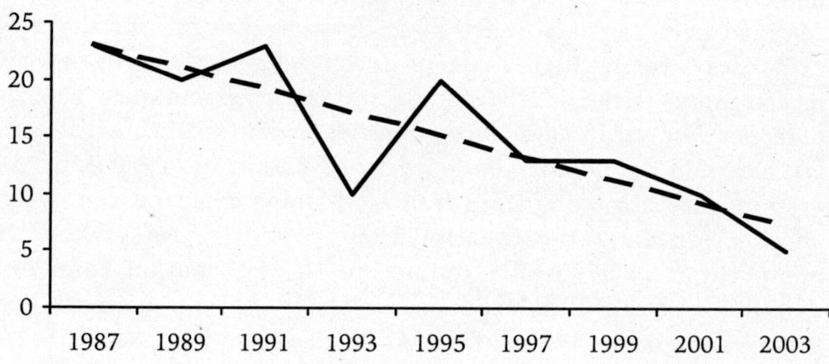

Source: WTO

Table 3.1

New Investigations and Impositions of Definite AD Measure 2000-2004

	2000	2001	2002	2003	2004	Average
Investigations	31	33	23	8	29	24.8
Impositions	51	12	28	5	11	21.4

Table 3.2 exhibits how new investigations by the EU are largely about exports from developing countries. In 2004, eighty six per cent of all new investigations concerned exports from developing countries. In 2003, the share was as high as 100 per cent. This is not a new development. For decades, anti-dumping investigations from the EU—and the United States—have mainly concerned developing country exports.

Table 3.2

New Investigations Initiated by Country of Export 2000-2004

	2000	2001	2002	2003	2004
Developing country	29	32	19	8	25
Developed country	2	1	4	0	4
Developing country Share of new investigations (%)	94	97	79	100	86

There are, of course, several explanations to this phenomenon. Some developing countries are non-market economies that employ market practices that are not conducive to the idea of free trade (defined here as the absence of state intervention). But the main explanation to the high share of developing countries in new EU investigations is the cost advantage in developing countries. The cost of labour is lower in developing countries than in the EU, which gives producers in developing countries an advantage in labour intensive production. Thus, companies from developing countries can overall keep lower market prices for their products. And when the competition is generally tougher in the EU market than in a developing country, the exporting company can or even must keep lower prices in the EU market than in their home-market.

Again, this practice has virtually nothing to do with harmful dumping or 'unfair' trade but is a normal market practice. Similarly, blocking these companies export opportunities by imposing anti-dumping duties, or forcing them to price undertakings, has nothing to do with protecting a fair trading order or protecting consumers. It is sheer protectionism.

The European Union and Anti-Dumping

Factors of political economy can explain much of the use of anti-dumping measures, in the European Union as well as in other countries. This does not mean that all anti-dumping actions are influenced by political considerations. As shown in a few recent research papers, the role of political influence in anti-dumping decisions are easy to observe in the EU as well as in the US, but it is not the only factor explaining the use of anti-dumping. Some cases are addressing dumping activities that are outright abuses of free trade. Another set of explanations, to some extent also taking stock against political economy factors, seems to concern macroeconomic variables and their influence on changes in prices. For example, if an economy is expanding there is likely to be an increase in demand. This would, *ceteris paribus*, likely raise the price of exporter's products and, thus, reduce the likelihood of dumping. Inversely, in a recession, where demand is falling, the price of the export product is likely to fall as the exporter try to retain the market share, and this increase the likelihood of dumping.

Changes in the relative price of a country's currency can also have the same effects and research seems to suggest that appreciations of the real exchange rate in the EU have a positive impact on the openings of anti-dumping procedures.

Although, not being the most notorious user of anti-dumping measures, the European Union has to take a lot of the blame for the contagion of anti-dumping measures that we have witnessed the last decades. In particular, since the EU has been prone to use anti-dumping measures to protect EU producers from fair competition—some even suggests that EU started this trend (especially anti-dumping actions against China, the country faced with the highest numbers of anti-dumping actions).

In principal, the EU is in favour of a reform of the anti-dumping practices and a WTO reform. However, that does not necessarily mean that the EU will stop using measures to curb exports from low-cost countries. As the recent developments in EU-China trade relations have shown, there are other methods to use if a country is really interested in diluting free trade. To manage change and adjustment, and to promote a 'redistribution' of trading shares for several countries in the developing world, were the arguments used by the EU Commission to defend the new quotas against Chinese textile exports.

This is perhaps a change in rhetoric, but not in practice.

4

Why is China the World's Number One Anti-Dumping Target?

YUEFEN LI

Introduction

The first anti-dumping investigation against China was launched by the European Community in 1979, immediately after China started opening its economy to the outside world. Since then, the filing of contingent protection measures targeted at China have proliferated at a rapid pace, with anti-dumping actions far more prevalent than other measures such as safeguards. In the 1980s, anti-dumping cases against China averaged 6.3 per year. The number increased to 30.3 per year in the 1990s. From 1996 up to the present day, China has ranked first in the world in anti-dumping investigations and final measures against its exports.

The cost of anti-dumping activities against Chinese exports is quite high. From 1979 up to October 2002, 33 countries initiated 544 anti-dumping and safeguard cases and measures against Chinese exports, affecting more than 4,000 products with a value of around US\$ 16 billion. However, this amounted to only about 5 per cent of China's total exports, and was not extensive enough to cripple the economy.

An analysis follows on the major factors contributing to China's position as number one target of anti-dumping investigations in the world over the past consecutive few years.

External Factors

Anti-Dumping Laws Could be Used to Benefit Multinational Enterprises and Victimise Late Industrialisers

As laws are not amended as frequently as developments take place, it is not uncommon for them to be manipulated and abused by contemporaries. However, when laws are too outdated, they may give rise to incidences of running counter to the very principles on which the law was introduced.

Many countries have amended their anti-dumping (AD) laws in recent years. The WTO Agreement on Anti-dumping was endorsed in 1994, only a relatively short time ago. However, some of the basic economic assumptions of international trade conducted in the 18th century are still the cornerstone of the AD laws. That is what a recent McKinsey study describes as a "residency-based view of trade," which means that exports are goods and services leaving a nation's borders, regardless of nationality and ownership of producers and service-providers involved, while imports are the mirror of exports. However, these basic assumptions no longer apply to a large part of international trade because of the tremendous changes that have occurred since the days of barter trade and the time when the first anti-dumping laws were introduced. Multinational enterprises (MNEs) have increasingly begun to offshore their production activities and trade between affiliates and their parent companies have mushroomed.

A significant proportion of the goods and services exported from a country do not really belong to that particular country. With FDI, companies no longer need to cross national borders to sell their products. A volume of cross-border trade directly associated with the determination of dumping action no longer accurately reflects actual commercial activities between two trading nations. Not to take these changes and factors into consideration in AD laws may result in the unwelcoming outcome of not meeting the intended purpose of legislators when they enacted the law. Anti-dumping duties were conceived in Canada at the beginning of the 19th century with the intention of maintaining a "level playing field" for domestic industries whose activities essentially took place within national frontiers. Subsequently, they were extended to cover transactions from outside the national borders. However, as pointed out by Richard J. Pierce Jr., globalisation and the rise of MNEs have meant that in many cases anti-dumping laws have been administered and manipulated to "facilitate the formation, maintenance, and enforcement of cartels."

One common feature of anti-dumping laws/agreements is that they have sufficient loopholes to allow MNEs to use them to squeeze out efficient new market rivals. This is one important reason why major newly-industrialising economies (NIEs) experienced a time when they were the targets of contingent protection measures; this came at a time when they underwent fast economic growth and foreign trade expansion, which quite often forced them to set up foreign direct investment (FDI) operations abroad. China has entered such a period, but has not yet developed the capacity to engage in large scale FDI to jump anti-dumping activities.

The internationalisation and segmentation of production chains and the rise of MNEs have rendered anti-dumping laws antiquated. On the whole, anti-dumping laws/agreements have placed countries that have few MNEs and countries that are new entrants to the global market at a very disadvantageous position. MNEs are demanders of export prices and also have the capability to collude against a particular product from a developing country; they do so by using contingent protection measures, creating instability and uncertainty for their exports such as reductions in trade volumes, losing market shares for their goods and, in some cases, withdrawing from the market totally. MNEs have used anti-dumping measures as an instrument to strengthen their monopoly.

The costs of anti-dumping measures on the domestic economies of the targeted countries in terms of financial losses and human suffering when workers are laid off are much larger for developing countries than for industrial countries. For the initiating countries, the protection it affords its domestic producers is limited. It is true that a number of developing countries, including China, have also become major initiators of anti-dumping investigations; however, more often than not, this was because domestic industries find it hard to adjust to a highly competitive environment. Without large MNEs, they are not in a position to use anti-dumping to create a monopoly in a certain market.

Dramatic changes have taken place in the global economy since the promulgation of the first anti-dumping law in Canada. The rise of MNEs and progress made in technology and communication has fundamentally changed the landscape of global production supply chains. Production is now globalised and segmented. Component and service inputs and assembly operations involved in the production of a traded product can now take place in different countries. The growing integration of national economies, a process known as globalisation, is mainly coordinated by MNEs through FDI and, to a lesser extent, by other contractual arrangements. An important part of FDI is market oriented which means that affiliates of MNEs sell products directly to host-country markets, thus jumping both tariff, non-tariff barriers including anti-dumping concerns. This renders outdated the concept of trade balance since it does not cover the goods and services sold by MNEs in FDI host countries, even though these can be very significant.

MNE affiliates in host countries are treated as residencies of these countries. Their local sales, regardless of whether they are goods or services, are not considered as exports and are, therefore, not included in the trade balance. In cases when these affiliates export goods and services produced in the FDI host-countries to their home-countries, they would be reflected in the trade balance as exports of the FDI host-country to the MNE affiliates' home-country. According to an article published by McCaughrin (2004) (see Figure 4.1):

> "Nearly three times as many goods are sold overseas by US foreign affili-ates as by US exporters. Incorporating foreign affiliate sales reduces the US deficit by almost a full percentage point of GDP. US multinationals are not alone in relying on affiliates to distribute goods overseas. Japanese multinationals exported $325bn of goods during the first three quarters of 2003. But on top of that, Japanese affiliates sold an additional $287bn of goods (excluding sales back to Japan) that are not captured in the trade balance."

So for the MNEs, in addition to the various incentives offered by the host countries, the goods and services sold directly in foreign markets by their affiliates are not included in the bilateral trade balance, thus minimising domestic political pressure on host countries to take contingent protection against them. This makes for a major criteria to impose contingent protection such as "material injury" to domestic producers, "import surge" and "market disruption" less relevant. Japanese FDI flows to the European Union and the United States in the 1980s were positively affected by the overall increase in the number of anti-dumping actions in the two jurisdictions. This may explain why Japan's position in the anti-dumping investigations league tables fell from its number one position for the period of 1981–1997 to the fourth position for the period of 1995–2001. In addition, once production facilities have been set up in these jurisdictions, they can file anti-dumping petitions under local anti-dumping laws against foreign rivals. China, being a developing country, still relies heavily on exports to promote its economic development.

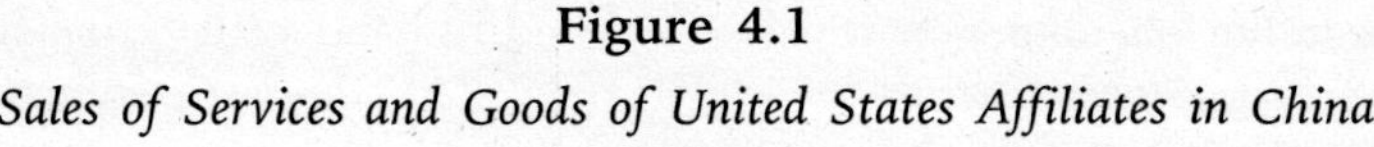

Figure 4.1

Sales of Services and Goods of United States Affiliates in China

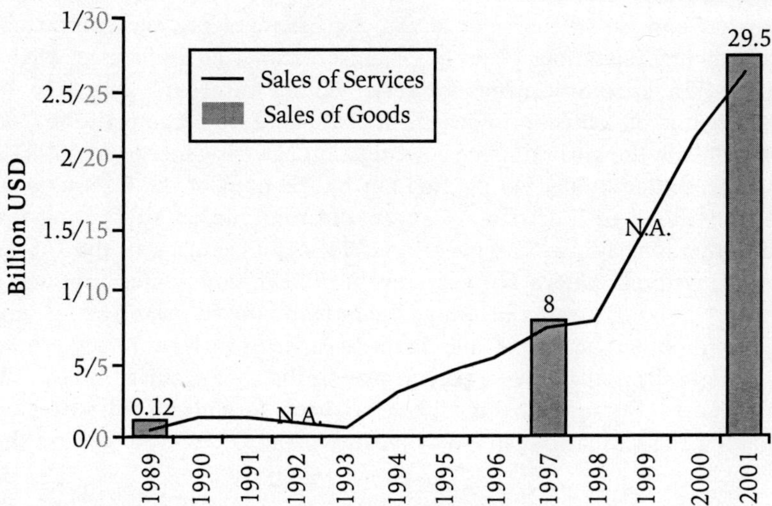

Sources: Bureau of Economic Analysis (www.bea.doc.gov)
Economic Policy Institute (www.epinet.org)

As MNEs have production facilities located in different parts of the world, they are also capable of dodging anti-dumping activities targeted at exports from their affiliates. For instance, if a MNE has had an affirmative anti-dumping ruling against products it has manufactured in China, the MNE could redirect the product to a market other than the one with anti-dumping restrictions in place against the product made in China. Meanwhile, its affiliate located in a third country can export the same product to the complaining country with a product originating from a country other than China. Thus, through trade diversion, the MNE could survive positive anti-dumping rulings without losing market share. In 2003, the United States threatened to levy dumping charges on some colour TV sets made in China, a company such as Philips exported large screen TVs assembled in China to the United States, its Chairman and Chief Executive said that the anti-dumping activity "do not affect Philips operations" as his company "could shift TV production to its Mexico plants" and export to the US market from there.

Another phenomenon which goes hand in hand with globalisation and growing interdependence is that, so-called "domestic industries" are, in many cases, no longer purely domestic. They very often have similar and varied ties with MNEs, e.g. shareholding and contractual assembling operations. They can even sometimes be affiliates of MNEs based in a complaining country. Vested interests give rise to suspicions of collusion to snatch market share from competitors. One example is the anti-dumping investigation against Chinese colour TVs in the United States. As pointed out by the head of the International Brotherhood of Electrical Workers, the trade union supporting the anti-dumping filing, "the majority of TV manufacturing in the U.S. is multinational. There are very few American companies producing TVs." Labour unions at Sanyo Manufacturing in Arkansas, Sharp Electronics in Tennessee and Toshiba America in New Jersey are all Japanese firms that have a part to play in the case against Chinese TV producers. Because of this, there has been "a widespread suspicion among the China industry that Japanese companies were behind the case."

MNEs, through their affiliates, often collude with each other to squeeze out new foreign market entrants, particularly new and weak entrants from developing countries. In 1998 Maur wrote that:

> "... collusion between firms operating in several countries and deciding to hit jointly a common foreign rival-especially when these firms do not occupy a dominant position in their respective markets could be another hypothesis for explaining multiple overseas petitions. We can imagine that MNE firms meeting in a specific market may agree to coordinate their strategies against a common rival. Some instances of "echoing" could support that hypothesis.

This explains why most NIEs are targets of anti-dumping activities or have experienced a period of intense trade friction with major industrialised countries. China is also going through a period of heavy reliance on foreign trade to promote economic growth and industrialisation. The table on ratio of share of anti-dumping investigations and share of export value shows that China's ratio of share of anti-dumping investigations is very high in relation to its share of world trade. This could support the hypothesis that it is a target of anti-dumping and that China is, in fact, faring worse than NIEs. According to its WTO accession agreement, China will continue to be treated as a non-market economy until 2016. China's non-market economy status makes it an even easier target of MNE collusion, as "surrogate values" for anti-dumping ruling are always

Table 4.1

*Ratio of Share of Anti-Dumping Investigations
and Share of Export Value*

	Share of Anti-Dumping Investigations in Total World Investigations (Per cent)				Export Share of Total World Exports (Per cent)				Ratio of Share of Anti-Dumping Investigations and the Share of Export Value			
	1981-1987	1988-1998	1998-2002	1981-2002	1981-1987	1988-1998	1998-2002	1981-2002	1981-1987	1988-1998	1998-2002	1981-2002
China	4.15	10.97	13.59	9.40	1.45	2.36	4.00	2.44	2.86	4.65	3.40	3.85
Japan	8.88	5.88	4.42	6.50	6.92	8.68	6.98	7.74	1.28	0.68	0.63	0.84
Republic of Korea	5.16	6.89	7.96	6.58	1.46	2.17	2.51	2.03	3.53	3.18	3.17	3.24
Taiwan Province of China	4.06	4.60	5.25	4.58	1.20	2.15	2.14	1.84	3.58	2.14	2.45	2.49
United States	8.71	8.53	4.36	7.64	14.63	11.76	11.90	12.70	0.60	0.73	0.37	0.60

Sources: UN Comtrade Database; WTO Anti-Dumping Gateway (*www.wto.org*); Zanardi (2002); UNCTAD Calculations.

obtained from a third party in "comparable market-economy countries." MNEs sometimes succeeded in getting companies related to the enterprises in the complaining country to provide surrogate values. Several studies documented cases of collusion against Chinese exports (Maur, 1998).

MNEs are also capable of creating a dumping scenario to take advantage of a protected market after a positive ruling of dumping. There were cases when foreign firms chose to increase the likelihood that trade barriers would be erected against its own industry, as this could be an optimal strategy if the firm could then shift production to the protected country and tariff jump thereby giving them the edge over competing foreign firms unable to engage in FDI. The mechanism is a simple one. When MNEs spot a new efficient entrant to the market, they purposely reduce their sales in that market in order to fabricate a proof of injury in the investigation stage of an anti-dumping petition. Then, after anti-dumping restrictive measure forced the new rival to withdraw from the market, they would re-enter the much more protected market. This is a strategic way for MNEs to maximise their profit margin and optimise their monopoly.

Globalisation has hastened the growth of buyer-driven commodity chains that connect advanced country marketing or retail companies with contractors manufacturing in low-cost developing economies. Very often the lead firm is a brand name merchandiser or a large retailer in a developed country which orchestrates the procurement, manufacture and marketing of products manufactured by contractors, and sub-contractors in developing countries. Because of China's cost advantages, in particular low labour cost, China has become an important downstream producer in these global commodity chains. However, one of the constant pressures facing those at the lower end of the commodity chain is the incessant demands by brand name merchandisers and large retail distributors for lower export prices. If these demands are not met the producers risk losing the contracts; and Chinese firms have little bargaining power as they depend on the demands of MNEs. As noted by Gereffi, the powerful influence of the lead firm in shaping contractor relations is indisputable.

By pressuring Chinese suppliers, these retailers and wholesalers may very well widen their profit margins. However, they also push Chinese suppliers into a very unpleasant anti-dumping petition. All the same, when it comes to anti-dumping investigations, the tendency would be to blame Chinese enterprises for taking away jobs of the complaining countries instead of wholesalers or retailers of the complaining country trying to optimise their bottom lines.

In a number of anti-dumping cases against Chinese enterprises, those enterprises involved were caught between the conflicts of the various domestic interests of the complaining country. Two recent anti-dumping cases inspired by the United States against Chinese wooden bedroom furniture and colour TV illustrate this. In the case for furniture, the United States Department of Commerce noted that the anti-dumping petition on Chinese wooden bedroom furniture has split the furniture manufacturing and retail industries as companies are taking sides in the political battle. The United States Furniture Retailer Association published an article on its website which reveals that the anti-dumping petition, to a large extent was a conflict between domestic forces (namely export interests *versus* import-competing interests) than a conflict between countries.

The rise of MNEs and four decades of trade liberalisation also render anti-dumping ineffective in protecting domestic industries. Indeed, anti-dumping measures can cost exporters dearly and can even totally exclude them from a market as shown by the European Union anti-dumping rulings against Chinese colour TVs and bicycles. Because of this, anti-dumping has risen in prominence as an instrument for imposing import restrictions. However, trade diversion from other producers can fill the vacuum within a very short period of time. Modern technology and communication, and segmentation of the production chain can all in one way or another facilitate the process. So what "the injured domestic producers" get from a positive ruling is mostly just a breathing space of very limited duration. On top of this, due to increasing interdependence, anti-dumping actions also have had a negative impact on other interest groups of the complaining country.

As demonstrated in the United States furniture case against China, wholesalers, retailers and wood exporters in the United States suffer at the same time as Chinese furniture manufacturers. The only beneficiaries are the United States furniture manufacturers. For exports with high import contents, the characteristic of Chinese exports, all of the parties involved in the production chain will, to some extent, be negatively affected by anti-dumping rulings. And as shown by the furniture case, more often than not, the type of trade restrictions seen today end up redistributing trade, disproportionately penalising one country while rewarding another, without necessarily achieving the original objective of protecting the industry intended.

Trade Liberalisation, Contingent Protection and
Newly Industrialising Economies

China's impressive expansion of international trade started in the late-1970s, when two decades of trade liberalisation had already resulted in considerably lower tariff levels in many countries. Since then further deepening of trade liberalisation has reduced significantly the importance of tariff as a trade barrier. As anti-dumping activities can be invoked relatively easily and selectively compared to other trade measures, and as anti-dumping investigations, regardless of the nature of their final rulings, can lead to almost immediate loss of market share on the part of exporting countries, they have also become the most frequently used trade remedies. By the 1990s anti-dumping had become a major instrument of trade protection for developed countries. Since the WTO Agreements went into effect in 1995, this instrument has become increasingly popular in all countries. So, while trade liberalisation opens doors for late industrialisers; anti-dumping, safeguard, and countervailing measures have also been used to deter or harass them, China in particular.

Both developed and developing country governments have been encouraging and supporting domestic producers to use anti-dumping as a mechanism to protect their markets. Developing countries started to enact anti-dumping laws and tried to raise awareness on anti-dumping practices. Developed countries have made anti-dumping activities more user-friendly. Some have even provided incentives to the users of anti-dumping measures. In the United States, amendments to anti-dumping law have made it easier for domestic firms to prove the existence of dumping, including extensions of the definition of "less than fair value" to include both international price discrimination and sales below cost. Moreover, the United States has a legislation, known as the Byrd Amendment, designed to give anti-dumping duties collected by the United States Customs Service to private companies that filed anti-dumping petitions. In the fiscal year 2003, United States Customs and Border Protection paid out US$190 million in Byrd Amendment claims. It is a *de facto* subsidy to anti-dumping petitioners, as indicated in the WTO ruling in April 2004.

Given this kind of international environment at a time when China was going through fast trade expansion, it is not surprising that it has become the world's number one target for anti-dumping activities. However, as we will see in the next section, China's specific trade and economic structure has also contributed to the skyrocketing of anti-dumping charges against its exports.

Domestic Factors Contributing to the Utilisation of Contingent Protection Measures Against Chinese Exports

From 1978 to 2002, China's exports increased around 12 per cent on a year-on-year basis – much higher than the world average (Figure 4.2). While it is not an unprecedented phenomenon, China's sharp increase of trade within a relatively short period of time is still quite remarkable. Not surprisingly, this event has given rise to increasing anti-dumping petitions. Currently, China's large bilateral trade surplus with the United States is a heated political topic in the United States and has led to allegations of currency manipulation and unfair trade practices. All this indicates that China has now entered a stage of intense trade frictions with some of its trading partners, as did Japan in the 1970s.

Figure 4.2

Trade Expansion in China from 1982–2003

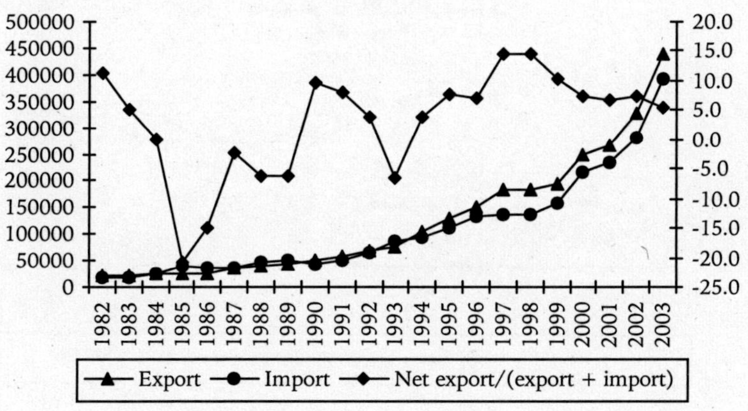

Source: IMF DOT, February 2005.

Note: Estimates for 2004 are based on the 9-month cummulative value of 2004 over the same period in 2003.

China's trade structure also makes it an easy target of trade protectionist measures. Exports are highly concentrated according to destinations. Although, great efforts have been made to diversify, progress has not been as fast as it could have been. The United States, Japan, European Union and Hong Kong (China) still account for 70 per cent of China's exports. For example, 75 per cent of China's textile and apparel exports are concentrated in five markets, i.e. Hong Kong (China), Japan, the United States, the European Union and the Republic of Korea. Another example is furniture export. According to official statistics, China produced nearly US$20 billion worth of furniture in 2002, of which one-third was exported, half of it to the United States. This high reliance on a few markets gives rise to anti-dumping pressure (see Figure 4.3).

Figure 4.3

Export Destinations

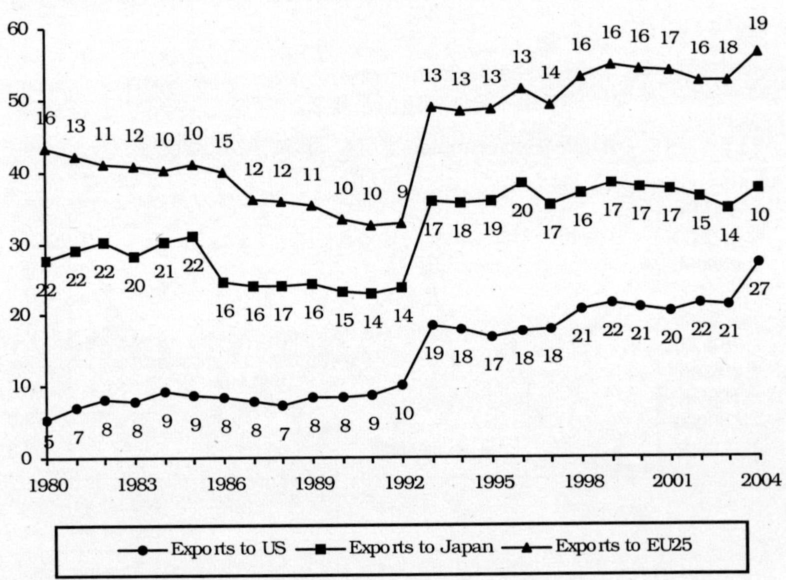

Source: IMF DOT February 2005.

Note: Estimates for 2004: based on the 9-month cummulative value of 2004 over same period in 2003.

As for export product categories, up to the first half of 1990s China's exports had the characteristics of an economy undergoing the initial stages of industrial development. There were almost no brand products and little high value added. Exports were mostly labour intensive and composed of standard and basic products. However, these were also the products of sunset industries in industrialised countries that have become the object of intensive/vigorous anti-dumping claims. Anti-dumping investigations can win time and allow market share for those industries in developed countries to adjust as this normally will take longer with protection. US anti-dumping investigations against Chinese steel went on for a whole year and even though the final verdict was in China's favour, the damage was done. Some customers were lost and the stocks of the Chinese enterprises involved went into free fall on the stock market.

According to a Chinese Government source, 70 to 80 per cent of the total anti-dumping investigations against China are concentrated on textiles, chemicals, steel and mineral sectors, all of which are labour intensive and low value added sectors of productivity. Most of these are the sunset industries in developed countries that are at the same time the mainstay industries for countries undergoing the first stages of industrialisation. In the past three years, chemicals and metals still ranked foremost for anti-dumping investigations. Messerlin found that anti-dumping measures in metals, chemicals, machinery and electrical equipment, textiles and clothing, and plastics accounted for 75 per cent of the total number of measures. He also noticed that these products are characterised by a high proportion of relatively standard production and oligopolistic structures. He suspects that complaining firms use anti-dumping as an instrument to segment the market and squeeze out new rivals.

Ironically, although China has been treated as a non-market economy by some of its trading partners, the diminishing role of government in production planning and the foreign trade has also led to duplicate investments and overcapacity. The government is no longer directly involved in foreign trade although it continues to monitor its operations at an arms' length. For most export products, the government's present function is to maintain a registry system. Manufacturers' associations have not acquired the capacity to influence production activities.

An increasing number of Chinese firms in the export sector are operating in a market environment where the purchase of inputs and the raising of finance are founded on commercial principles. Exporting enterprises, however, have yet to learn to operate more systematically– i.e. by conducting feasibility studies and business planning. Herd behaviour is prevalent; once a producer enters a major market, many others follow. In the process, not much attention has been paid to the overall volume and value increase in the export market. These huge increases do easily trigger anti-dumping petitions. Thus, there is still a lot to learn for the government to perfect its use of fiscal, financial, legal and administrative measures that are allowed by WTO rules in order to guide the economy maintain a rational and balanced increased rate of fixed asset investments and so secure a stable and sustained development of the foreign trade sector.

Many exporting companies lack a good understanding of WTO Rules of Origin. As a result, the 'Made in China' label was placed on exports which were, in fact, not really up to the threshold set by the Rules of Origin. This consequently has artificially boosted the actual volume of Chinese exports. With this working environment, the education of exporters and the enforcement of such rules should in principle form part of the government's responsibilities.

In addition, the majority of enterprises resort to price competition for market entry and market expansion in both domestic and international markets. Product upgrading and differentiation is yet to be utilised as a tool to capture and maintain market share. A significant part of Chinese exports is still concentrated in such anti-dumping intensive products as textiles, clothing, footwear and travel items. One important reason for this phenomenon is that most of these products have low market entry cost. As product upgrading requires research and development and the recovery of this kind of sunk cost will take time, companies tend to avoid this type of strategic investment. Instead, there is a tendency for domestic entrepreneurs to rush to produce the same products at about the same time, thereafter creating a highly competitive situation. More often than not, exports are priced at extremely low levels with razor thin profits. Some anti-dumping charges may have been well substantiated because intense price competition in China may push enterprises into periods of selling at a loss.

China's heavy concentration of export destinations as well as its dramatic expansion of trade is closely related with the rising importance of processing trade. Unlike Japan and the Republic of

Korea which emphasised the development of their national brands and their own national giants with horizontal and vertical production specialisation, i.e. with the entire production process undertaken within their countries, China's trade expansion has relied heavily on processing trade.

From 1979 to the end of 2003, processing trade grew 243-fold. Since 1995 processing trade has been the most important mode of foreign trade in China. Presently around 50 per cent of China's exports are processed (Figure 4.4). While there is a deficit under normal trade, China's total trade surplus mainly comes from processing trade—processing of imported materials accounts for three quarters of this trade while the remainder is taken up by the processing of material provided by foreign importers of the eventual finished products.

Figure 4.4

Trend of Processing Trade

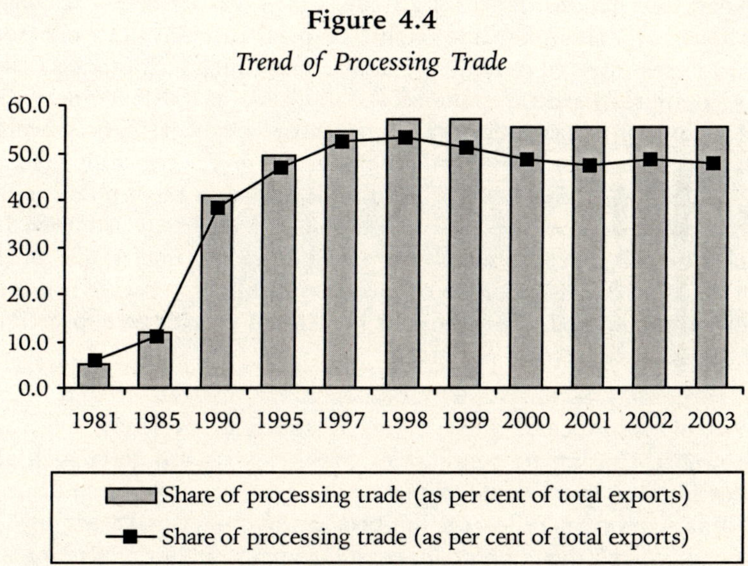

Source: General Administration of Customs of China.

Processing trade was started by companies in Asian NIEs. Most of them were small-scale companies which concentrated on labour-intensive goods, including goods that were anti-dumping intensive and from sunset sectors. This reflects the famous flying geese model of development with early industrialisers moving up the production ladder and passing on the traditional sectors to the latecomers. While upgrading their exports from standard basic products into more differentiated products, Hong Kong (China), Japan, Singapore, the Republic of Korea, and Taiwan Province of China transferred some of their traditional and anti-dumping intensive operations into China where labour and infrastructure costs were relatively cheap. This transfer has provided China with the badly needed job opportunities and has also extended product life cycles and profit margins by cutting production costs. This arrangement represents a win-win situation for both China and NIEs. One drawback, however, is that it is prone to trade disputes.

Around the mid-1990s, the processing trade in China entered into a different stage. This has had a profound change on its export compositions but seemed to further accentuate the imbalance in export destinations. Processing trade, which was formerly exclusively labour-intensive, became rather capital-intensive as overseas businesses invested heavily in manufacturing high-tech products such as computer hardware, chemicals and auto parts. Machinery and electronic products now contribute to over half of China's overall exports and about 70 per cent of the entire processing trade volume. This does not mean China's technological level in these products has reached the competitive levels of developed countries. It is rather that the Chinese firms are mainly responsible for the final stages of the production, a division of labour characterised by lower-wage countries for lower-end production, whereas higher-end activities are focused on countries where costs are higher.

According to the Ministry of Commerce, in 2003 around 80 per cent of the processing trade was financed by overseas investors. However, the import contents of these exports are quite high and mostly come from Asian countries. The production of these firms in China, however, relies on imports of machineries to set up the operation, and then imports parts and components for processing and final assembly. While Chinese workers earn a tiny share of the total value of the products in the form of wages, multinational firms are making handsome profits out of these activities. A major source of imports for assembling and re-exporting are from Asian economies. This type of "vertical specialisation" in the production process in the Asian region has resulted in China acquiring an increasingly important role in the final assembly stages of a broad range of export commodities. It has also intensified the heavy reliance United States and European Union markets – the traditional export destinations for Asian exports.

Trade volume between China and the United States accounted for 5.4 per cent of China's GDP in 1997, but rose to 8.95 per cent in 2003. China is the source for the increasing share of goods exported to United States markets. These same goods were those previously produced by Japan, Taiwan Province of China, Singapore, the Republic of Korea and Hong Kong (China). As a result, China has been running big trade deficits with some Asian economies at the same time that it was experiencing a growing surplus with the United States. Some economists call this trade pattern as the "relocation of deficits."

> "The effect of 'relocation of deficits' can best be illustrated by the US trade deficits in electronic products, which increased from US$50.4 billion in 1998 to US$88.8 billion in 2002. This group of products is also important because the US deficit in these products with China came up to as much as US$31.4 billion in 2002, more than one-third of the Sino-US total trade deficit registered in US official figures.... Apparently, US deficits in electronics with China grew by US$17.0 billion during 1998-2002. However, US deficits with Japan decreased by US$7.1 billion and those with Taiwan fell by US$1.5 billion. The 'relocation of deficits,' thus, constituted more than a half of the increase in Sino-US trade imbalance in electronic products.

As a result, the increased trade surplus has been far from being proportionate to the increase of the trade volume. The size of current account balance has been declining over the last few years up to 2002. Proportionately, in 2002, the weight of the current account surplus over the entire balance of payments has reduced by close to 40 per cent in comparison with the situation in 2000.

China's WTO accession protocol states that the country may be treated, on a case-by-case basis, as a non-market economy (NME) for anti-dumping purposes until 2016. The issue of whether or not it is fair to regard China as a NME is not the subject of this paper. However, it needs to be said that being categorised as an NME greatly increases the possibility of a positive dumping ruling and places China at a disadvantage. With this clause in China's accession protocol, the burden to prove "less than normal value" and "material injury" would be much lighter. As a matter of fact, it has also given rise to abuse as production costs can be calculated according to those that are from a surrogate country. Since the surrogate country had not been chosen by the Chinese, it has often transpired that the countries that were chosen were places where material and labour costs were much higher than in China, which definitely do not lay the foundation for a fair assessment in anti-dumping cases. There are opportunities to manipulate data which in greater likelihood result in a positive ruling of a case. In addition, an assessment of this kind of data could also result in much higher dumping margins, and lead to higher punitive anti-dumping duties. There is also a domino effect as the whole process can be executed relatively easily and the chances of success are high, this in turn leads to a higher level of anti-dumping incidences.

The lack of legal capacity on the part of Chinese enterprises to respond to anti-dumping investigations abroad is also a factor contributing to the frequency of final anti-dumping measures against Chinese exports. In the past, most of the Chinese exporters were unaware of the anti-dumping process. So, when their products were accused of being dumped, their first response was bewilderment and panic. When they learnt of the cost of anti-dumping litigations, they invariably pulled out. As a result, no-response and absentee rulings were quite common, which means affirmative injury ruling was almost a certainty. The lack of qualified staff with good knowledge of the language of the country bringing the case and anti-dumping practice also prevented Chinese enterprises from defending their interests. In this situation the vulnerability of Chinese farmers is unparalleled because most of them are still not aware about dumping and anti-dumping practices. In addition, China had never had any producer/manufacturers' associations before, nor did it have powerful and effective interest groups which can be found in industrialised countries. When each enterprise fought its own battle, their strength definitely could not match their foreign counterparts.

"Echoing" anti-dumping investigations happen very often to China. When a complaint was filed in one country, producers in other countries quickly followed suit. The absence of an immediate response from China after an anti-dumping petition has been filed and the ease with which a positive ruling could be obtained encourages competitors to free ride. This is not only because of fear of trade diversion; it is also a strategic response in order to reduce future competition by eliminating a rival.

The United States and European Union have for many years topped the list of those submitting anti-dumping cases against China. However, as China's exports are highly concentrated in these markets, China does not have much leverage against anti-dumping investigations originating in these markets. Chinese retaliation against anti-dumping activities has been very measured for fear of upsetting major importers, and has, thus, never constituted a strategic threat to them. The absence of built-in counter-force and credible threat to these markets has placed China at the receiving end of trade restrictive measures. However, with the increase in recent years of both FDI inflows and exports from the United States into China, the situation has, to some degree, been mitigated. China has now even filed anti-dumping cases against the United States.

Prusa (2002) has pointed out that countries generally have significant discretion in the use of anti-dumping law because of the way in which anti-dumping statutes are drafted. Thus, countries and individual industries within countries have learned that they can use the laws to their advantage in a variety of ways. So if politically and strategically China-bashing during a United States election year is to their advantage, there would be more anti-dumping activities against China. It has been a routine practice to increase trade frictions between the United States and China every election year.

Even though the total number of anti-dumping investigations initiated worldwide has decreased over the past two years, some large developing countries, including China, have increased their use of anti-dumping mechanism. China is also a target of anti-dumping investigations from developing countries. Since 2002, India has replaced the United States as the number one country in launching anti-dumping investigations against Chinese exports. On average, anti-dumping duties from developing countries are higher than those imposed by industrial countries. One example is Mexico which levied punitive tariffs on Chinese footwear as high as 1,105 per cent.

It needs to be pointed out although there is a fundamental difference between anti-dumping activities between those initiated by the developing countries and developed countries. Developing countries have little capacity to engage in FDI to jump anti-dumping. Nor do these countries have latitude to collude with MNEs to squeeze out new rivals. These countries' major concern is to protect domestic producers since it is not possible to rely on tariff protection *vis-à-vis* widespread trade liberalisation. Developing countries neither have the financial capacity to provide domestic support or subsidies to the same degree as the developed countries.

There are two important reasons behind the increasing anti-dumping investigations from developing countries against Chinese exports. Firstly, developing countries, with the support of their governments, become more aware of anti-dumping procedures. Secondly, being at the same stage of development and with exports coming from similar traditional sectors increases the factor that developing countries may be at loggerheads with one another not only in some international but also in domestic markets. Thirdly, the blatant double standard of developed countries in dumping heavily subsidised agricultural products into developing countries and beyond, and their abuse of anti-dumping have made developing countries think they too have to play the same game.

Conclusion

There have been a number of criticisms about the methodology used to determine dumping, particularly with regard to its opaqueness and the resulting ease of manipulation. For many years, developed countries have been heavy users of anti-dumping activities to protect their sunset industries, and their MNEs have used anti-dumping as a weapon to strengthen monopoly rather than to enhance a "level playing field." The inherent weakness and loopholes of anti-dumping laws are among the reasons why China is a target of anti-dumping activities, as it is a new and relatively efficient new rival in the world market. The WTO members are currently negotiating within the Negotiation Group on Rules to further clarify and improve the Agreement on Anti-Dumping. According to the Doha Ministerial Declaration which was adopted on 14 November 2001, the ongoing negotiation is "aimed at clarifying and improving disciplines" instead of changing the basic concepts and principles, which means anti-dumping activities will continue to have an important impact on international trade.

The present stage of development and development model of the People's Republic of China has determined that in addition to expanding its domestic consumption, trade expansion is as essential for its economic growth. Its trade structure, with the increasing importance of processing trade, may provide the badly needed job opportunities. This may also allow for the relocation of some sunset industrial sectors, and consolidate and expand the existing heavy concentration of export destinations. Although, China's export composition has undergone drastic changes, its role as an assembler and final stage producer does place it at a disadvantage when it comes to anti-dumping activities. In the long run, however, it is necessary for China to shift its export products away from anti-dumping-intensive sectors by upgrading export products from standard products into highly differentiated products. The development of China's own brand of products, and undertaking a horizontal production for some important dynamic products can also minimise exposure to foreign anti-dumping charges against Chinese exports and thereby reduce financial losses. In view of the cost of anti-dumping to the economy, it is now time for China to put into place a screening mechanism as permitted by the WTO accession conditions before engaging itself in new processing trade deals.

The extensive safeguard provisions that are included in China's WTO accession commitments could constrain China's export growth. Moreover, intensified anti-dumping activities against Chinese exports will not only be detrimental to China's trade balance; it will also hurt the world. China's track record for trade and economic performance has shown that the benefits of its trade expansion have been distributed much more broadly than have done some earlier NIEs. This is because in a globalising world, China's exports rely heavily on foreign capital, imports of primary, intermediary and capital goods.

References

Farrell D., Ghai S. and Shavers T. (2005). "A Silver Lining in the US Trade Deficit." *The McKinsey Quarterly*, March 2005, various pages.

Frenkel S. (2001). "Globalisation, Athletic Footwear Commodity Chains and Employment Relations in China." *Organisation Studies*, 22(4). ABI.INFORM Global.

Gereffi G., Palpacuer F., and Parisotto A. (1999). *Global Production and Local Jobs.* International Labour Office, Geneva, Switzerland.

Harney A. (2004). "Chinese Factories Roll-out More Perks to Woo Workers." *Financial Times*. 19 March.

Maur J.C. (1998). *Echoing Anti-dumping Cases, Regulatory Competitors, Imitation and Cascading Protection.* Groupe d'Economie Mondiale & Institute d'Etudes Politiques de Paris.

McCaughrin R. (2004). "Dispelling Trade Myths," *Global Economic Forum.* Morgan Stanley, 5 April. In http://www.morganstanley.com/GEFdata/digests/20040405-mon.html#anchor1

Messerlin P.A. (2002). "China in the WTO: Anti-dumping and Safeguards." *American Economic Review* 2602.

Miranda J., Torres R. and Ruid M. (1998). "The International Use of Anti-dumping: 1987–1997." *Journal of World Trade*, 32(5):5–71.

Nolan P. and Zhang Jin (2002). "The Challenge of Globalisation for Large Chinese Firms." *UNCTAD Discussion Papers*, No. 162, July. Geneva, United Nations Conference on Trade and Development.

Pierce R.J. Jr. (1999). "Anti-dumping Law as Means of Facilitating Cartelisation." *Public Law and Legal Theory Working Paper 002*, George Washington University Law School.

Prusa T.J. and Skeath S. (2002). *Retaliation as an Explanation for the Proliferation of Anti-dumping*. Rumbaugh T and Blancherm N (2004). "China: International Trade and WTO Accession," *IMF Working Paper*, WP/04/36. Washington, DC, International Monetary Fund.

United States, *International Trade Administration*, Department of Commerce. Fact Sheet.

Vandenbussche H.R., Veugelers and Belderbos R. (1999). *Undertakings and Anti-dumping Jumping FDI in Europe*.

WTO (2004). World Trade Organisation *Press Releases*, various issues.

Zanardi M. (2004). "Anti-dumping: What are the Numbers to Discuss at Doha?" *World Economy*, 27(3), 403-433.

5

Time to Dump Certain Anti-Dumping Provisions?

Looking Through the Dispute Settlement Mechanism Proceedings

DEBASHIS CHAKRABORTY

Introduction

Much has been discussed about the WTO-incompatibility of Anti-Dumping procedures of various countries in the trade policy literature. The WTO agreement on anti-dumping (henceforth ADA), which allows member countries to impose anti-dumping duties (henceforth ADD) as a contingency measure, and not as a protectionist mechanism, has often failed to limit it to that extent. In fact, it has evolved as a mechanism to provide protectionist cover for the domestic industries. The improper usage of this provision has often highlighted the need to reform the WTO agreement (Lindsey and Ikenson, 2002; Raju, 2004). It has been noted from time to time that there exist several loopholes in the provision, through which a country can practice protectionist measures (Banik, 1998; Debroy and Banik, 2000). In the current period, concerns have been raised at times over the increasing use of these provisions in a trade-distorting manner (Aggarwal, 2004).

The true globalisation of the anti-dumping measures is fast emerging as a major problem in the recent period, and there is an urgent need to respond to this tendency. While in the earlier period the usage of this provision was not so frequent among the developing countries, the trend has changed during recent years. We will get back to this point in an Indian context later in our analysis. The *WTO Annual Report* (2003) notes, "The increasing use of contingency measures, particularly anti-dumping actions, is also a key area of interest to Members. Although, the upward trend was somewhat reversed in 2001, when the number of new anti-dumping measures in force fell to 159 from 235 in the previous year, this is still considerably greater than the numbers imposed in 1995, 1996 and 1997. More Members, including developing countries, are resorting to them increasingly. The rising trend in the use of such measures prompted Members to place the matter on the DDA." However, as discussed in the following, the problems are far from being over.

The effectiveness and rationale of anti-dumping procedure in order to curb cheaper imports, marketed at a supposedly 'unfair' price, is questionable. It has been shown in the subsequent analysis that while initiating the investigations and imposing final duties, the 'home government' often does not conform to the WTO norms. In a significant number of cases, the imposition of ADD has been proved WTO-incompatible (see Table 5.1 in the following). There is no doubt about the fact that the dumping procedure ends up hurting the interest of the consumers. In this scenario, a serious debate should follow on urgent modification, and in the extreme case, the rationale behind continuation of certain provisions of ADA under the wings of WTO.

The paper is organised along the following lines. First, we briefly discuss the WTO cases on anti-dumping lodged at DSB and several observations, as reflected from them, are noted. On the basis of these observations, we further focus on the major sub-articles, which are mainly causing the problems for the exporting countries. The relevant information for the analysis is obtained from the recent DSB update (WTO, 2005). Then we look into the anti-dumping cases involving India, and the changing perspective of the country in this issue. Finally, on the basis of the observations, some future concerns are noted.

A Global Scenario

First we focus on the cases lodged at the DSB, and by analysing the alleged violations made in the submissions by the appellant; an attempt is made to identify the potential areas of conflict. The article-level analysis is summarised in Figure 5.1. It is observed that maximum number of disputes are lodged questioning the imposition of article 5 (concerning initiation procedures and subsequent investigation) and article 2 (determination of dumping), followed by article 3 (determination of injury to domestic industry) and article 6

Figure 5.1

Alleged Violation of Anti-Dumping Agreement — Article-wise

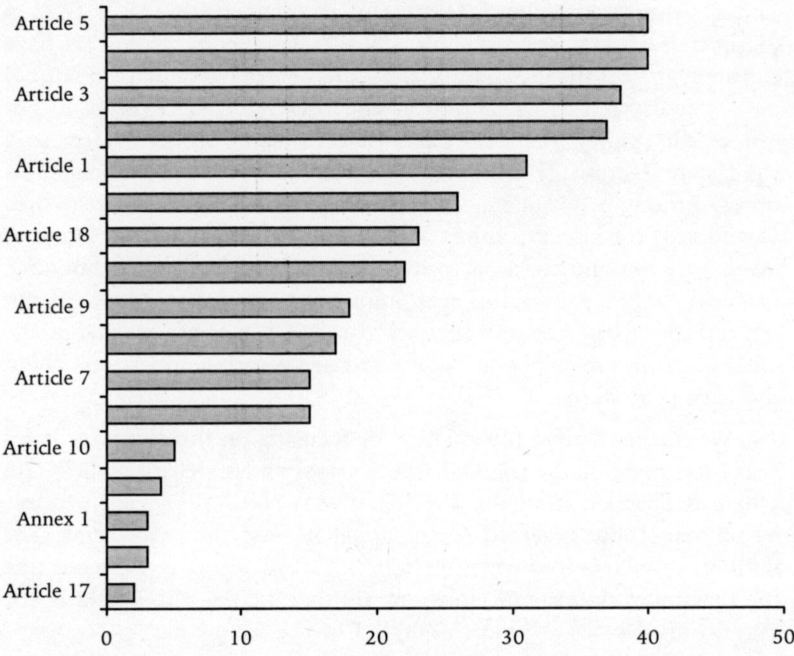

(concerning evidence) respectively. The high incidence of DSB cases on these categories speaks out the potential of mishandling of anti-dumping cases on these grounds, which actually covers almost the entire procedure. Indeed the determination of 'dumping' and estimating the 'injury' has been a major bone of contention. Other ADA provisions attracting disputes are article 1 (conformity of applied procedures with the ADA), article 12 (public notification of the procedures and explanation of the determinations), article 18 (procedures relating to final provisions) and annex II (determination on the basis of best information available when collecting direct evidence is a problem). It has been alleged by affected countries at times that the notification procedure, a much-needed measure for ensuring transparency, is seldom properly followed. Furthermore, the clause 'best available information' is subject to various interpretations, and could be utilised by any country to tilt the result of the investigation in its favour. Further, down the list, alleged violation takes place on the grounds of article 9 (imposition and collection of ADD), article 11 (duration and review of ADD and price undertakings), article 7 (provisional measures) and article 4 (definition of domestic industry). While the affected exporters have claimed at various occasions that the imposition of provisional measures as well as the duration and review of ADD often do not reflect the reality, the very basis of the initiation, i.e., harm to a significant section of 'industry' (article 4), has been challenged at times. Among other alleged violations, article 15 (special regard to developing countries), annex I (procedures regarding on the spot investigations) and article 8 (price undertakings) deserve mentioning. In short, only a handful of less important articles in ADA did not attract any alleged violation over the last ten years, showing the misuse of the provisions at large and raising serious questions about the very procedure.

We further extend the analysis by focusing on the measures ruled WTO-incompatible by the DSB (both panel and appellate bodies). An article is dropped from the analysis if it is ruled WTO-incompatible by the panel, but reversed by the appellate body and vice versa. The findings are illustrated with the help of Figure 5.2. It is observed that the maximum number of violations till date by any sub-article is six. The observations are briefly analysed in the following:

1.   First, article 2.4 ('fair comparison' between export price and normal value), article 3.4 (consideration of 'all relevant economic factors' for determination of dumping) and article 6.8 (final determination on the basis of 'available facts') are declared WTO-incompatible maximum number of times. These three clauses, taken together, shows that the determination of the dumping margin and the investigation procedure is often not in line with the obligation of members under WTO. In line with article 6.8, violations on Annex II (determination on the basis of best information available when collecting direct evidence is a problem) are also quite high, as attested by the DSB, five times. Especially, non-market economies have suffered most from this provision.

2.   Second, the determination related concerns, i.e., article 3.1 (examination of the impact of dumped imports on prices of domestic 'like products' and their producers), article 3.2

Figure 5.2

Actual Violations of Anti-Dumping Agreement — DSB Rulings

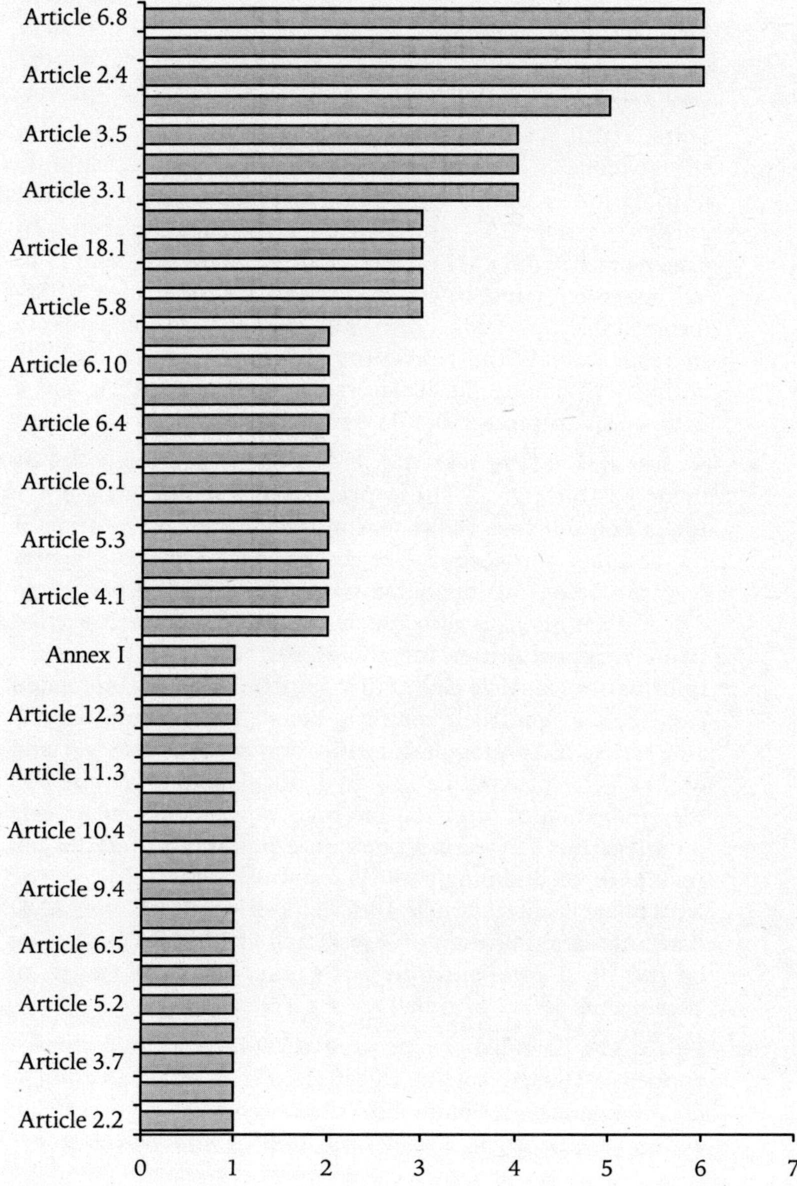

(investigation on significant increase in dumped imports and price undercutting) and article 3.5 (demonstration of causal relationship between dumped import and injury) have been declared WTO-incompatible four times each. This shows that the investigations initiated are not often backed by necessary background works by the home country. In other words, the inclination towards imposition of ADD has been too evident.

3. Third, article 5.8 (immediate termination of investigations in the absence of sufficient evidence), article 12.1 (public notification of sufficient evidence to reach the interested parties), article 18.1 (imposition of no specific action in disagreement with GATT 1994) and article 18.4 (adoption of 'all necessary steps' to conform with ADA) are ruled WTO-incompatible three times each. Absence of WTO-compatibility in terms of all the four provisions attests the lack of enthusiasm among the violators to conform to ADA, and a willingness to protect the domestic industry.

4. A number of provisions have been declared WTO-incompatible twice. These provisions include article 4.1 (definition of domestic producers), article 5.3 (examination of the accuracy and adequacy of the evidence provided), article 6.2 (providing full opportunity to all interested parties to defend their interests throughout the investigation), article 6.4 (timely opportunities for all interested parties to see all information), article 6.9 (full opportunity to all interested parties to defend their interests before final determination) and article 12.2 (detailed notification of the findings) and others. The provisions violated once include article 3.7 (determination of threat on the basis of facts, and not merely on allegation, conjecture or remote possibility), article 5.2 (evidence of dumping, injury and their causal link in the written application), article 10.4 (imposition of definitive ADD only after determination of threat) and article 11.2 (reviewing of the need for continuing the duty after the lapse of 'reasonable period of time').

5. Finally, the potential of practicing WTO-incompatibility under various WTO-agreements, as reflected from the DSB rulings, are summarised in Figure 5.3. It is observed that government actions under article 3 (determination of injury to domestic

Figure 5.3

The Distribution of Violations of ADA as per DSB Ruling

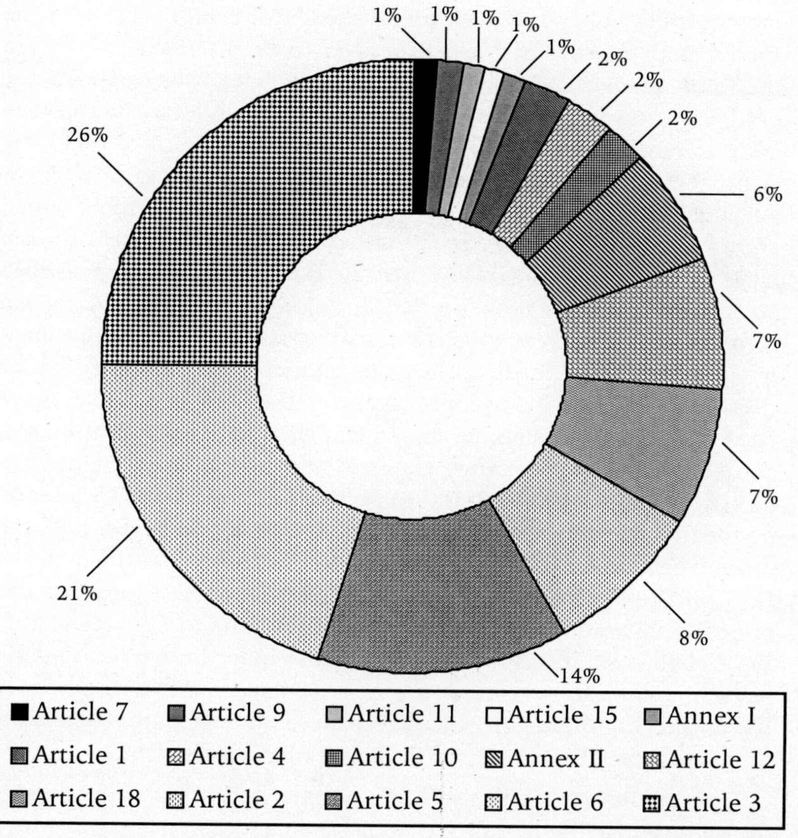

industry – 26%), article 6 (the procedures concerning evidence – 21%), article 5 (relating to initiation procedures and subsequent investigation – 14%) and article 2 (determination of dumping – 8%) have been proved WTO-incompatible most frequently. In short, this puts a question mark on the entire process of dumping determination mechanism.

To have an overall assessment of the trends in ADA cases, we present the outcome of the complaints lodged at DSB under seven different categories in Table 5.1, following the framework devised by Chakraborty and Chaisse (2005). In the first two columns, we present 'win' and 'loss' in a particular case. We define 'win' by a complainant if it wins at the panel level, even if the appellate body reverses certain legal interpretations of the verdict later, since the existence of a WTO-incompatible policy has been established. However, rejection of the claims, both at panel and appellate body level, is termed as 'loss'. In the third column, under the head 'continuing', we have clubbed three options – cases with ongoing review, cases currently with the appellate body and cases where verdict is expected within a specified time. The fourth option deals with the joint request of the parties to DSB for suspension of proceeding after the panel has been formed, which shows that either of the two sides is willing to negotiate on the alleged measures in force. Fifth, we note the cases where no panel had been formed, which show mutual discussion, probably leading the respondent to guarantee the desired market access for the complainant to resolve the dispute. Two other possibilities cannot be ruled out in this case. First, (if a developed country) the complaint might have been raised for harassing the respondent as a trade policy instrument, and second, (if a developing country) the complainant might have lacked the necessary technical expertise to support his claim, and decided to opt out before formation of the panel. Sixth, we note the cases where a mutually agreeable solution has been notified to the DSB. In the final column the cases where the alleged measure was promptly discontinued after the initial notification at DSB are placed. We feel that an analysis of this column is quite important. On one hand, this indicates the existence of WTO-incompatible measures in force, and highlights the effectiveness of the dispute settlement mechanism on the other as a credible threat mechanism.

The results of the analysis are summarised in Table 5.1. Apart from looking at the overall scenario, we also focus on the US, which is the largest violator of the provision (in terms of cases lodged against it). From the overall scenario reported in the upper panel, we see that every third case lodged at the DSB has represented a valid concern, i.e., the existence of WTO-incompatibility of the provision in question has been proved. Only in two occasions, the complaints have been defeated. Six cases are currently continuing. There has been no request to suspend the panel proceeding on the issue of dumping till date, and on one occasion amicable settlement has been notified to the WTO. In a large number of cases (twenty-five), no panel has been formed. Finally, on three occasions, the respondent has removed the alleged WTO-incompatible measure (DS 23 – involving Venezuela as

Table 5.1

An Analysis of DSB Complaints

Year	Overall							
	A	B	C	D	E	F	G	Total
1996	1	0	0	0	1	1	1	4
1997	1	0	0	0	1	0	1	3
1998	4	0	0	0	1	0	0	5
1999	4	0	0	0	4	0	0	8
2000	3	0	0	0	4	0	0	7
2001	4	1	0	0	4	0	0	9
2002	2	1	0	0	3	0	0	6
2003	0	0	4	0	2	0	0	6
2004	0	0	2	0	5	0	1	8
Total	19	2	6	0	25	1	3	56

Year	Countries Complaining against United States' Anti-Dumping Policies							
	A	B	C	D	E	F	G	Total
1996	0	0	0	0	1	1	0	2
1997	1	0	0	0	0	0	1	2
1998	1	0	0	0	0	0	0	1
1999	3	0	0	0	0	0	0	3
2000	1	0	0	0	0	0	0	1
2001	2	1	0	0	2	0	0	5
2002	2	1	0	0	2	0	0	5
2003	0	0	3	0	0	0	0	3
2004	0	0	1	0	3	0	0	4
Total	10	2	4	0	8	1	1	26

Constructed from Dispute Settlement Updates, WTO (2005).

respondent, DS 89 – involving the US as respondent and DS 313 – involving the EC as respondent) after initial request for consultation was made to the DSB.

The analysis involving the US as respondent has been reported in the lower panel of Table 5.1. It is observed that almost 50 per cent of the total number of cases relating to ADA has been lodged against it. Since the analysis is done on the basis of complaints, column A represents the cases, where the US practices has been defeated. Column B on the other hand represents the scenario when the US policies in question were ruled WTO-consistent by the WTO. Two points deserve particular mention. First, it is observed that US accounts for more than 50 per cent of the cases where the policies of the importing country have been ruled WTO-incompatible. Second, only the US has been able to twice win a case as respondent (DS 221 – involving Canada as appellant, DS 244 – involving Japan as appellant).

The analysis carried so far indicates gross violation of the ADA procedures and consequent worsening of consumer welfare in the importing country. Given this trend, we focus on the anti-dumping cases involving India (both as an appellant as well as respondent) in the following.

Anti-Dumping Disputes Involving India: A Review of Issues

Before going into the discussion of anti-dumping cases, a comparative analysis of the two Trade Policy Review reports on India will not be irrelevant here. While the earlier review (1998) has been critical of India on various accounts like tariff reform, import restriction procedures, absence of full compliance with TRIPS, lack of liberalisation of domestic service sectors etc., the last review (2002) praised the reform measures already undertaken during the inter-survey years. The concerns raised over India's unfinished reform agenda in the 2002 review were not too many in number, but it identified the increasing trend in anti-dumping investigations as one of the major future concerns:

> "India has become one of the major users of anti-dumping measures, with some 250 cases initiated since 1995... Moreover, the number of anti-dumping measures in force has risen steadily, especially since 1997, from 19 notified measures in force, to 131 in 2001 (Chart III.3). The majority of the initiations have been for chemical and related products (47.2%); a large number of actions have been initiated against imports from the European Union (19.2%) and China (18.8%)."

In general, the increasing usage of anti-dumping procedures by India has caught the attention of the international community. The WTO Annual Report (2004) notes, "Of the 1323 measures in force reported, 21% were maintained by the United States, 16% by India, 15% by the European Communities, 7% each by South Africa and Canada, and 6% by Argentina. Other Members reporting measures in force each accounted for 5% or less of the total." Since the publication of the 2002 review, India has faced three cases as respondent, all of which have been filed on the working of the anti-dumping procedures.

In particular, the recent request by EC for consultation on imposition of anti-dumping measures in India on 27 commodities (DS 304), followed by complaints of Bangladesh (DS 306) and Taiwan (DS 318) shows the seriousness of the claims. The results of these three cases would have profound implication for all future cases against India in this area. The US and even China has occasionally raised concerns over the frequent initiations of anti-dumping investigations in India. However, as seen through the excerpt from the annual report (2003-04) of the Directorate General of Anti-Dumping and Allied Duties provided below, the India claims that its procedures are in line with the relevant WTO provisions, although the three complaints testify otherwise.

> "The national legislation in respect of anti-dumping was put in place when the Customs Tariff (Identification, Assessment and Collection of duty or Additional duty on Dumped Articles and for Determination of Injury) Rules, 1985 were notified. Sections 9, 9A, 9AA, 9B and 9C of the Custom Tariff Act, 1975 as amended in July 1995 and the Customs Tariff (Identification, Assessment and Collection of Anti-Dumping Duty on Dumped Articles and for Determination of Injury) Rules,1995 as amended (in July 1999 vide Notification No.44/1999; in May 2001 vide notification No.28/2001, in January 2002 vide Notification No.1/2002 of 4th January 2002 *and in November 2003 vide Notification No. 101/2003-customs(Non-Tariff) dated 10.11.2003)* and Customs Tariff (Identification, Assessment and Collection of Countervailing Duty on Subsidised Articles and for Determination of Injury) Rules, 1995 framed there under form the legal basis for anti-dumping and anti-subsidy investigations and for the levy of anti-dumping and countervailing duties. These laws are in conformity with the WTO's Agreement on implementation of Article VI of the GATT 1994, commonly known as Agreement on Anti-Dumping and Agreement on Subsidies & Countervailing Measures."

Table 5.2 notes the evolution of India in the global scenario of anti-dumping investigations, where the cases faced and imposed by three countries, EU, India and the US are compared. While in the initial years after WTO formation, the initiations by India were not so high, it increased steadily upto June 1999, but declined in the subsequent period. However, the investigations increased from July 2000 onwards, and have surpassed the number of investigations initiated by the EU and the US during the last two periods noted. Furthermore, in Table 5.3, we summarise the last three cases lodged against India, in order to analyse the problems associated with the procedures followed. Since no panel report has been released on these cases till date, we look at the alleged violations as reported in the table. The alleged violations common in all three cases are article 1 (conformity of applied procedures with the ADA), article 3.1

Table 5.2

A Comparison of Anti-Dumping Cases between EU, India and the US

	India		EU		US	
	A	B	A	B	A	B
1 January 1995 – 31 December 1995	5	3	33	21	13	6
1 January 1996 – 31 December 1996	20	10	23	35	21	21
1 January 1997 – 31 December 1997	13	7	41	59	16	15
1January 1998 – 31 December 1998	33	12	21	42	22	15
1 January 1999 –30 June 1999	40	6	32	20	28	7
1 July 1999 – 30 June 2000	27	11	49	32	29	10
1 July 2000 – 30 June 2001	37	-	29	-	77	-
1 July 2001- 30 June 2002	76	12	23	39	58	11
1 July 2002 – 30 June 2003	67	12	15	32	29	12

Source: WTO Annual Reports (various issues).

A – Anti-dumping investigations initiated by the country;

B – Anti-dumping investigations initiated against the country.

(examination of the impact of dumped imports on prices of domestic 'like products' and their producers), article 3.2 (investigation on significant increase in dumped imports and price undercutting), article 3.5 (demonstration of causal relationship between dumped import and injury), article 6.8 (final determination on the basis of 'available facts'), article 6.9 (full opportunity to all interested parties to defend their interests before final determination), article 12.2 (detailed notification of the findings) and annex II.

In Table 5.4, experience of the seven cases involving India as complainant has been summarised. In the last case (DS 313 – involving the EC), the measures at issue, in violation with articles 3.4, 3.5, 4.1 and 9.2 of the ADA were withdrawn after India moved to the DSB, which could be termed as a success. On three occasions (DS 229 – involving Brazil, DS 168 – involving South Africa, DS 140 – involving the EC), no panel has been formed although India alleged major violations in the working of the anti-dumping investigations in each case. On the remaining three occasions, the DSB bodies have ruled in India's favour. In DS 141 (involving EC) although the panel rejected several claims made by India, the measures applied by EC were ruled WTO-inconsistent on the ground of article 2.4 ('fair comparison' between export price and normal value), article 3.4

Table 5.3

India at the DSB on Anti-Dumping Issues as Respondent

Case No.	Complainant	Alleged Violation	WTO Ruling
DS 318 (2004)	Separate Customs Territory of Taiwan, Penghu, Kinmen and Matsu	The provisional and definitive anti-dumping measures imposed by India on the seven chemical and related products are inconsistent with – • Article VI:1 and VI:2 of GATT 1994 • Articles 1, 2, 3.1, 3.2, 3.3, 3.4, 3.5, 3.7, 3.8, 4, 5, 6 (including Annex II), 7.4, 12.1 and 12.2 of the ADA	Consultation in progress.
DS 306 (2004)	Bangladesh	The Anti-Dumping measures are inconsistent with - • Articles I:1 and II:1; Article VI in cluding Articles VI:1, VI:2 and VI:6(a) and Articles XXIII:1(a) and XXIII:1(b) of GATT 1994 • Articles 1, 2.1, 2.2, 2.4, 3.1, 3.2, 3.3, 3.4, 3.5, 3.7, 5.4, 5.8, 6.2, 6.4, 6.5, 6.8 (including para. 3 of Annex II), 6.9 and 12.2 of the Anti-Dumping Agreement.	Consultation in progress.
DS 304 (2003)	European Communities	The Anti-Dumping measures are inconsistent with - • Article VI:1 of GATT 1994 • Articles 1, 3.1, 3.2, 3.5, 6.6, 6.8 (including Annex II), 6.9 and 12.2 of the Anti-Dumping Agreement.	Consultation in progress.

(consideration of 'all relevant economic factors' for determination of dumping) and article 15 (developing country concerns). In DS 206 (involving the US), despite getting most of the claims rejected, India was able to prove WTO-inconsistency of certain US policies. Finally in DS 217 (involving US), the US procedures were ruled WTO-incompatible with article 5.4 (support to the application by domestic industry), article 18.1 (imposition of no specific action in disagreement with GATT 1994) and article 18.4 (adoption of 'all necessary steps' to conform with ADA). It is interesting to note that the violations faced by India in foreign markets (both developed and developing) and the alleged violations made by it are mostly different.

Table 5.4

India at the DSB on Anti-Dumping Issues as Complainant

Case No.	Respondent	Alleged Violation	WTO Ruling
DS 313 (2004)	European Communities	The EC measure is inconsistent with – •1 Articles 3, especially Articles 3.4 and 3.5; 4.1 and 9.2 of ADA	EC has agreed to terminate the measure at issue, and both parties have notified DSB of the mutual solution. No Panel formed.
DS 229 (2001)	Brazil	The measures on Indian jute bags are inconsistent with – •1 Articles VI and X of GATT 1994 •2 Articles 1, 2, 3, 5, 6 (especially 6.6, 6.7, 6.8 and Annex II, 6.9, 6.10), 11, 12, 17.6(i), 18.3, 18.4 of the ADA •3 Article XVI of the WTO Agreement	
DS 217 (2001)	United States	The amendment to the Tariff Act of 1930 signed on 28 October 2000 with the title of "Continued Dumping and Subsidy Offset Act of 2000" (known as "the Byrd Amendment") is inconsistent with – • Article 18.1 of the ADA in conjunction with Article VI:2 of the GATT and Article 1 of the ADA • Article 32.1 of the SCM Agreement, in conjunction with Article VI:3 of the GATT and Articles 4.10, 7.9 and 10 of the SCM Agreement • Article X(3)(a) of the GATT • Articles 5.4, 8 and 18.4 of the ADA • Articles 5, 11.4, 18 and 32.5 of the SCM Agreement	The Panel found that the CDSOA was inconsistent with – • Articles 5.4, 18.1 and 18.4 of the ADA • Articles 11.4, 32.1 and 32.5 of the SCM • Articles VI:2 and VI:3 of the GATT 1994 • Article XVI:4 of the WTO Agreement However it rejected the claim that CDSOA was inconsistent with – • Articles 8.3 and 15 of the ADA • Articles 4.10, 5 (b) 7.9 and 18.3 of the SCM • Article X:3(a) of the GATT 1994 The Appellate Body upheld most of the major conclusions of the Panel.

Contd...

...Contd...

Case No.	Respondent	Alleged Violation	WTO Ruling
DS 206 (2000)	United States	The procedures under US anti-dumping and countervailing duty law were inconsistent with – •1 Articles VI and X of the GATT 1994 •2 Articles 1, 2, 3 (especially 3.3), 5 (especially 5.8), 6 (espe-cially 6.8), 12, 15, 18.4 and Annex II of the ADA •3 Articles 10, 11 (especially 11.9), 15 (especially 15.3), 22 and 27 (especially 27.10) of the SCM Agreement •4 Article XVI of the WTO Agreement	Although, the panel rejected India's claims re-lating to Articles 6.8, 15 and paragraphs 3, 5, and paragraph 7 of Annex II of the ADA, it concluded certain US practices to be WTO-in-compatible.
DS 168 (1999)	South Africa	Anti-Dumping Duties on the Import of Certain Pharmaceutical Products from India are inconsistent with – •1 Articles 2, 3, 6(a) to (c) individually and in conjunction with 12, 12 and 15 of the ADA •2 Articles I and VI of GATT 1994	No Panel formed.
DS 141 (1998)	European Communities	The Anti-Dumping Duties on Imports of Cotton-Type Bed-Linen are inconsistent with – •1 Articles 2.2.2, 3.1, 3.2, 3.4, 3.5, 5.2, 5.3, 5.4, 5.8, 6, 12.2.2, and 15 of the ADA •2 Articles I and VI of the GATT 1994	Although, the panel rejected India's claims re-garding Articles 2.2, 2.2.2, 3.1, 3.4, 3.5, 5.3, 5.4, and 12.2.2 of the ADA, it ruled that EC acted inconsistently with its obligations under Articles 2.4.2, 3.4, and 15 of the same Agree-ment. Later India won a case on the failure of the EC to bring its policy in line with its WTO obligation within the reasonable time.
DS 140 (1998)	European Communities	Anti-Dumping Investigations Regarding Unbleached Cotton Fabrics are inconsistent with – •1 Articles 2.2.1, 2.4.1, 2.4.2, 2.6, 3.3, 3.2, 3.4, 3.5, 4.1(I), 5.2, 5.3, 5.4, 5.5, 5.8, 6.10, 7.1(I), 7.4, 9.1, 9.2, 12.1, 12.2 and 15 of the ADA •2 Articles I and VI of GATT 1994	No Panel formed.

Apart from direct involvement, India has at times participated in the DSB process as an interested third party. We note India's participation in that capacity in Table 5.5. It is interesting to observe that in all the four cases mentioned in the table, the US has been the respondent. The interest in the cases involving the US probably originated from the fact that India fought two cases with the latter as respondent. However, it deserves mention that the results of the cases are quite diverse. While in two cases, the US policies were ruled WTO-incompatible (DS 136 and DS 162 – involving the EC and Japan; DS 234 – involving Canada and Mexico), in the other two the DSB ruled that the complaints failed to establish their claims (DS 221 – involving Canada; DS 244 – involving Japan).

Apart from the DSB cases, a number of Indian export items are subject to anti-dumping investigations in the export markets, and the issues are highlighted from time to time (ESCAP, 2000). Recently, the debate over shrimps with US has come to forefront. Last year, U.S. International Trade Commission (USITC) imposed ADD on shrimp imports from India and Thailand. However, USITC is now considering withdrawal/revision of this duty owing to the changed conditions stemming from the December 2004 tsunami disaster.

In this background, India's negotiating strategy on anti-dumping at the WTO need to be focused. The negotiating strategy of India has so far been a combination of defensive as well as proactive strategies, and stressed on ensuring special and differential treatment for developing countries as well as revision of the ADA at the earliest. In the post-Doha period, India was focusing more on modification of the ADA for relaxing several provisions for developing countries, which clearly was not the right solution. While revision of the floor levels, as depicted in the paragraphs below, does not provide a permanent solution, it technically acknowledges the occurrence of dumping from developing countries (at least on some occasions)!

1. "The existing *de minimis* dumping margin of 2 per cent of export price below which no anti-dumping duty can be imposed (Article 5.8), needs to be raised to 5 per cent for imports from developing countries.

2. The threshold volume of dumped imports which shall normally be regarded as negligible (Article 5.8) should be increased from the existing 3 per cent to 5 per cent for imports from developing countries. Moreover, the stipulation

Table 5.5

Select Cases Involving India in DSB as Third Party

Case No.	Complainant	Respondent	Dispute	Results
DS136 and DS162	EC and Japan	United States	Anti-dumping Act of 1916	The Panel concluded that the US has acted inconsistently with Articles VI:1, VI:2 and XVI:4 of the GATT 1994 and Articles 1, 4.1, 5.1, 5.2, 5.4, 18.1 of the ADA. The Appellate Body upheld all of the findings and conclusions of the panel.
DS 221	Canada	United States	Section 129(c)(1) of the Uruguay Round Agreements Act	The Panel concluded that Canada had failed to establish that section 129(c)(1) of the Uruguay Round Agreements Act was inconsistent with Articles VI:2, VI:3 and VI:6(a) of the GATT 1994; Articles 1, 9.3, 11.1 and 18.1 and 18.4 of the AD Agreement; Articles 10, 19.4, 21.1, 32.1 and 32.5 of the SCM Agreement; and Article XVI:4 of the WTO Agreement.
DS234	Canada and Mexico	United States	Continued Dumping and Subsidy Offset Act of 2000	The Panel found that the CDSOA was inconsistent with Articles 5.4, 18.1 and 18.4 of the ADA, Articles 11.4, 32.1 and 32.5 of the SCM, Articles VI:2 and VI:3 of the GATT 1994 and Article XVI:4 of the WTO Agreement. However, it rejected the claim that CDSOA was inconsistent with Articles 8.3 and 15 of the ADA, Articles 4.10, 5 (b) 7.9 and 18.3 of the SCM and Article X:3(a) of the GATT 1994. The Appellate Body upheld most of the major conclusions of the Panel.
DS 244	Japan	United States	Sunset review of anti-dumping duties on corrosion-resistant carbon steel flat products from Japan	The Panel rejected all of Japan's claims challenging various aspects of the US laws and regulations regarding the conduct of "sunset" reviews of anti-dumping duties under US law. Although, the Appellate Body reversed four of the Panel's legal findings, they concluded that the US had acted WTO-consistently.

that anti-dumping action can still be taken even if the volume of imports is below this threshold level, provided countries which individually account for less than the threshold volume, collectively account for more than 7 per cent of the imports, should be deleted.

3. The lesser duty rule shall be made mandatory while imposing an anti-dumping duty against imports from developing-country Member by any developed-country Member."

In the subsequent period, India modified its stance to some extent and asked for reform in article 5.4 (lower limit on the proportion of domestic production affected by dumping), article 2.2.2 (procedure for collecting cost and profit data), 2.4.2 (procedures for establishing margins of dumping), article 3.4 (consideration of all relevant economic factors for examining the impact of dumping), article 3.5 (demonstration of injury by dumped imports), article 3.8 (application of anti-dumping measures with special care), article 6.8 (final determination on the basis of 'available facts'), article 11 (Duration and Review of Anti-Dumping Duties and Price Undertakings) and finally annex II (determination on the basis of best information available when collecting direct evidence is a problem). The potential of applying WTO-incompatible policies in terms of these articles have already been mentioned earlier. However, the focus on special and differential treatment has been revisited at times. At the General Council session on 24 July 2003, India proposed a specific short-term dispensation in favour of developing countries in the form of a grace period of two years during which no anti-dumping investigations on imports of textile and clothing products from developing countries shall be initiated. Supporting this demand in the following period, India explained the massive impact of dumping on its domestic industries to the WTO:

> "Reinforcing the protectionist motivation was also the fact that, in several instances, investigations into the same products were revived back-to-back, extending over long periods. In the case of one product (cotton fabrics), these were continued for five years. In the case of another (bed linen), these have been going on in one form or the other since January 1994."

The Way Ahead

The messy state of affairs in this field has been best summarised by Messerlin (2001), who notes, "There is no anti-dumping provision in GATS and—following the disastrous experience of anti-dumping in goods—one can only hope that there will never be." As already mentioned earlier, the increasing usage of this provision urged the members to place this concern at the Doha ministerial (2001), and subsequently the Doha Ministerial Declaration (paragraph 28) noted:

"In the light of experience and of the increasing application of these instruments by members, we agree to negotiations aimed at clarifying and improving disciplines under the Agreements on Implementation of Article VI of the GATT 1994 and on Subsidies and Countervailing Measures, while preserving the basic concepts, principles and effectiveness of these Agreements and their instruments and objectives, and taking into account the needs of developing and least-developed participants. In the initial phase of the negotiations, participants will indicate the provisions, including disciplines on trade distorting practices, that they seek to clarify and improve in the subsequent phase."

However, the discussions and negotiations failed to improve the scenario and the concerns were once again raised at the Cancun Ministerial (2003). The Cancun Ministerial Declaration (paragraph 7) noted that:

"We instruct the Negotiating Group on Rules to accelerate its work on anti-dumping and subsidies and countervailing measures, including fisheries subsidies, with a view to shifting its emphasis from identifying issues to seeking solutions."

Following the heavy criticism on the Derbez draft, negotiations were stalled, and when resumed again in July 2004, the anti-dumping provision was clearly not the focus of the meeting. It is highly unlikely that the concern will be *effectively* addressed in the Hong Kong Ministerial (2005) in December either.

Given the experience on anti-dumping investigations, there is an urgent need to look into the modification of the procedure, and the current analysis attempts to identify the potential candidates for future reform. It seems from the massive violations in the ADA that in future the continuation of the mechanism itself should be questioned. However, it is unlikely, at least as of now, that the members would agree to get rid of this mechanism. Therefore, the focus of the future negotiations should be on reform of the articles in ADA, which leave rooms for various interpretations for fulfilling protectionist purposes, and on limiting the use of the very mechanism itself. The identified 'misused' articles in Figure 5.2 are strong candidates for that purpose. Last but not the least, tackling the increasing trend of anti-dumping investigations in the developing countries should be a priority area, since the consumers in those locations get affected much more severely than their counterparts in developed countries in the entire process.

References

Aggarwal, Aradhna (2004). "Developing Countries and the WTO Anti-dumping Code: Issues and Suggestions," in Bibek Debroy and Mohd. Saqib (Ed.) *Future Negotiation Issues at WTO: An India-China Perspective*, pp. 345-377, Globus Books, New Delhi.

Almstedt Kermit and Norton Patrick (2000). "China's Anti-Dumping Laws and WTO Anti-Dumping Agreement" (Including Comments on Chain's Early Enforcement of its Anti-Dumping Laws), *Journal of World Trade*, 34(6), pp. 75-113.

Banik, Nilanjan (1998). "Anti-Dumping Measures – An Indian Perspective," *RGICS Working Paper Series*, No. 1, Rajiv Gandhi Institute for Contemporary Studies: New Delhi.

Chakraborty, Debashis and Julien Chaisse (2005). "Trade Policy Review Mechanism and Dispute Settlement System: A Cross-Country Analysis of Enforcing WTO Rules between Negotiations and Sanctions," in Bibek Debroy and Md. Saqib (Ed.) *WTO at Ten: Looking Back to Look Beyond*, pp. 210-278, Konark Publishers: New Delhi.

Debroy, Bibek and Nilanjan Banik (2000). "The Dumping Issue," *Global Business Review*, 1(1), pp. 75-90.

Economic and Social Commission for Asia and the Pacific (2000). "Non-Tariff Measures with Potentially Restrictive Market Access Implications Emerging in a Post-Uruguay Round Context," Studies in Trade and Investment, No. 40, United Nations: New York.

Government of India, *India and the WTO*, The Monthly Newsletter of Ministry of Commerce (various issues), Ministry of Commerce: New Delhi.

————. (2004). *Annual Report of Directorate General of Anti-Dumping and Allied Duties – 2003-04*, Ministry of Commerce: New Delhi.

————. (2003). "Anti-dumping Actions in the Area of Textiles and Clothing: Proposal for a Specific Short-Term Dispensation in Favour of Developing Members Following Full Integration of the Sector into GATT 1994 from January 2005," Submitted by India, *WTO Document No. WT/GC/W/502* (Document No. 14 July 2003).

————. (2002a). "Proposals on Anti-Dumping Agreement," Submitted by India, *WTO Document No. TN/RL/W/26* (Dated 17 October 2002).

————. (2002b). "Proposals on Implementation related Issues and Concerns," Submitted by India, *WTO Document No. TN/RL/W/4* (Dated 25 April 2002).

Irwin, Douglas A. (2002). *Free Trade under Fire*, Princeton University Press: Princeton, New Jersey.

Khan, Amir Ullah (2001). "Dumping Procedures: Looking Into the Issues" in the seminar on *The New WTO Round: Is Free Trade Fair Trade?*, jointly organised by Rajiv Gandhi Institute for Contemporary Studies and Liberty Institute, October 12, New Delhi.

Lindsey, Brink and Dan Ikenson (2002). "Reforming the Anti-Dumping Agreement: A Road Map for WTO Negotiations," *Trade Policy Analysis No. 21*, Cato Institute: Washington D.C.

Messerlin, Patrick A. (2001). "Anti-Dumping and Trade Remedies: A Necessary Reform," in Klaus Gunter Deutsch and Bernhard Speyer (Ed.) *The World Trade Organisation Millennium Round: Freer Trade in the Twenty-First Century*, pp. 148-160, Routledge: London and New York.

Raju, K.D. (2004). "Future of Anti-Dumping: Call for Reform," in the Conference on *Looking Beyond Cancun: The Trend in Trade Talk*, organised by Rajiv Gandhi Institute for Contemporary Studies and Liberty Institute, March 24, New Delhi.

MVIRDC (1994), *GATT Agreements: Final Text of Uruguay Round*, World Trade Centre: Mumbai.

US Government Documents, "Dumping Duties on Shrimp from India, Thailand Under Review," April 25, 2005, http://canberra.usembassy.gov/hyper/2005/0425/epf103.htm

World Trade Organisation, *WTO Annual Report* (Various issues), WTO: Geneva.

————. (2005). "Update of WTO Dispute Settlement Cases," *WTO Document No. WT/DS/OV/ 23* (Dated 7 April 2005), WTO: Geneva.

————. (1998). "India," *Trade Policy Review*, WTO: Geneva.

————. (2002). "India," *Trade Policy Review*, WTO: Geneva.

APPENDIX

The WTO Anti-Dumping Agreement

*Agreement on Implementation of Article VI
of the General Agreement on Tariffs and Trade 1994*

Members hereby *agree* as follows:

PART I

Article 1: Principles

An anti-dumping measure shall be applied only under the circumstances provided for in Article VI of GATT 1994 and pursuant to investigations initiated and conducted in accordance with the provisions of this Agreement. The following provisions govern the application of Article VI of GATT 1994 in so far as action is taken under anti-dumping legislation or regulations.

Article 2: Determination of Dumping

2.1 For the purpose of this Agreement, a product is to be considered as being dumped, i.e. introduced into the commerce of another country at less than its normal value, if the export price of the product exported from one country to another is less than the comparable price, in the ordinary course of trade, for the like product when destined for consumption in the exporting country.

2.2 When there are no sales of the like product in the ordinary course of trade in the domestic market of the exporting country or when, because of the particular market situation or the low volume of the sales in the domestic market of the exporting country, such sales do not permit a proper comparison, the margin of dumping shall be determined by comparison with a comparable price of the like product when exported to an appropriate third country, provided that this price is representative, or with the cost of production in the country of origin plus a reasonable amount for administrative, selling and general costs and for profits.

2.2.1 Sales of the like product in the domestic market of the exporting country or sales to a third country at prices below per unit (fixed and variable) costs of production plus administrative, selling and general costs may be treated as not being in the ordinary course of trade by reason of price and may be disregarded in determining normal value only if the authorities determine that such sales are made within an extended period of time in substantial quantities and are at prices which do not provide for the recovery of all costs within a reasonable period of time. If prices which are below per unit costs at the time of sale are above weighted average per unit costs for the period of investigation, such prices shall be considered to provide for recovery of costs within a reasonable period of time.

> 2.2.1.1 For the purpose of paragraph 2, costs shall normally be calculated on the basis of records kept by the exporter or producer under investigation, provided that such records are in accordance with the generally accepted accounting principles of the exporting country and reasonably reflect the costs associated with the production and sale of the product under consideration. Authorities shall consider all available evidence on the proper allocation of costs, including that which is made available by the exporter or producer in the course of the investigation provided that such allocations have been historically utilised by the exporter or producer, in particular in relation to establishing appropriate amortisation and depreciation periods and allowances for capital expenditures and other development costs. Unless already reflected in the cost allocations under this sub-paragraph, costs shall be adjusted appropriately for those non-recurring items of cost which benefit future and/or current production, or for circumstances in which costs during the period of investigation are affected by start-up operations.

2.2.2 For the purpose of paragraph 2, the amounts for administrative, selling and general costs and for profits shall be based on actual data pertaining to production and sales in the ordinary course of trade of the like product by the exporter or producer under investigation. When such amounts cannot be determined on this basis, the amounts may be determined on the basis of:

(i)   the actual amounts incurred and realised by the exporter or producer in question in respect of production and sales in the domestic market of the country of origin of the same general category of products;

(ii) the weighted average of the actual amounts incurred and realised by other exporters or producers subject to investigation in respect of production and sales of the like product in the domestic market of the country of origin;

(iii) any other reasonable method, provided that the amount for profit so established shall not exceed the profit normally realised by other exporters or producers on sales of products of the same general category in the domestic market of the country of origin.

2.3   In cases where there is no export price or where it appears to the authorities concerned that the export price is unreliable because of association or a compensatory arrangement between the exporter and the importer or a third party, the export price may be constructed on the basis of the price at which the imported products are first resold to an independent buyer, or if the products are not resold to an independent buyer, or not resold in the condition as imported, on such reasonable basis as the authorities may determine.

2.4   A fair comparison shall be made between the export price and the normal value. This comparison shall be made at the same level of trade, normally at the ex-factory level, and in respect of sales made at as nearly as possible the same time. Due allowance shall be made in each case, on its merits, for differences which affect price comparability, including differences in conditions and terms of sale, taxation, levels of trade, quantities, physical characteristics, and any other differences which are also demonstrated to affect price comparability. In the cases referred to in paragraph 3, allowances for costs, including duties and taxes, incurred between importation and resale, and for profits accruing, should also be made. If in these cases price comparability has been affected, the authorities shall establish the normal value at a level of trade equivalent to the level of trade of the constructed export price, or shall make due allowance as warranted under this paragraph. The authorities shall indicate to the parties in question what information is necessary to ensure a fair comparison and shall not impose an unreasonable burden of proof on those parties.

2.4.1 When the comparison under paragraph 4 requires a conversion of currencies, such conversion should be made using the rate of exchange on the date of sale, provided that when a sale of foreign currency on forward markets is directly linked to the export sale involved, the rate of exchange in the forward sale shall be used. Fluctuations in exchange rates shall be ignored and in an investigation the authorities shall allow exporters at least 60 days to have adjusted their export prices to reflect sustained movements in exchange rates during the period of investigation.

2.4.2 Subject to the provisions governing fair comparison in paragraph 4, the existence of margins of dumping during the investigation phase shall normally be established on the basis of a comparison of a weighted average normal value with a weighted average of prices of all comparable export transactions or by a comparison of normal value and export prices on a transaction-to-transaction basis. A normal value established on a weighted average basis may be compared to prices of individual export transactions if the authorities find a pattern of export prices which differ significantly among different purchasers, regions or time periods, and if an explanation is provided as to why such differences cannot be taken into account appropriately by the use of a weighted average-to-weighted average or transaction-to-transaction comparison.

2.5 In the case where products are not imported directly from the country of origin but are exported to the importing Member from an intermediate country, the price at which the products are sold from the country of export to the importing Member shall normally be compared with the comparable price in the country of export. However, comparison may be made with the price in the country of origin, if, for example, the products are merely trans-shipped through the country of export, or such products are not produced in the country of export, or there is no comparable price for them in the country of export.

2.6   Throughout this Agreement the term "like product" ("produit similaire") shall be interpreted to mean a product which is identical, i.e. alike in all respects to the product under consideration, or in the absence of such a product, another product which, although, not alike in all respects, has characteristics closely resembling those of the product under consideration.

2.7   This Article is without prejudice to the second Supplementary Provision to paragraph 1 of Article VI in Annex. I to GATT 1994.

Article 3: Determination of Injury

3.1   A determination of injury for purposes of Article VI of GATT 1994 shall be based on positive evidence and involve an objective examination of both (a) the volume of the dumped imports and the effect of the dumped imports on prices in the domestic market for like products, and (b) the consequent impact of these imports on domestic producers of such products.

3.2   With regard to the volume of the dumped imports, the investigating authorities shall consider whether there has been a significant increase in dumped imports, either in absolute terms or relative to production or consumption in the importing Member. With regard to the effect of the dumped imports on prices, the investigating authorities shall consider whether there has been a significant price under-cutting by the dumped imports as compared with the price of a like product of the importing Member, or whether the effect of such imports is otherwise to depress prices to a significant degree or prevent price increases, which, otherwise, would have occurred, to a significant degree. No one or several of these factors can necessarily give decisive guidance.

3.3   Where imports of a product from more than one country are simultaneously subject to anti-dumping investigations, the investigating authorities may cumulatively assess the effects of such imports only if they determine that (a) the margin of dumping established in relation to the imports from each country is more than *de minimis* as defined in paragraph 8 of Article 5 and the volume of imports from each country is not negligible, and (b) a cumulative assessment of the effects of the imports is appropriate in light of the conditions of competition between the imported products and the conditions of competition between the imported products and the like domestic product.

3.4   The examination of the impact of the dumped imports on the domestic industry concerned shall include an evaluation of all relevant economic factors and indices having a bearing on the state of the industry, including actual and potential decline in sales, profits, output, market share, productivity, return on investments, or utilisation of capacity; factors affecting domestic prices; the magnitude of the margin of dumping; actual and potential negative effects on cash flow, inventories, employment, wages, growth, ability to raise capital or investments. This list is not exhaustive, nor can one or several of these factors necessarily give decisive guidance.

3.5   It must be demonstrated that the dumped imports are, through the effects of dumping, as set forth in paragraphs 2 and 4, causing injury within the meaning of this Agreement. The demonstration of a causal relationship between the dumped imports and the injury to the domestic industry shall be based on an examination of all relevant evidence before the authorities. The authorities shall also examine any known factors other than the dumped imports which at the same time are injuring the domestic industry, and the injuries caused by these other factors must not be attributed to the dumped imports. Factors which may be relevant in this respect include, *inter alia*, the volume and prices of imports not sold at dumping prices, contraction in demand or changes in the patterns of consumption, trade restrictive practices of and competition between the foreign and domestic producers, developments in technology and the export performance and productivity of the domestic industry.

3.6 The effect of the dumped imports shall be assessed in relation to the domestic production of the like product when available data permit the separate identification of that production on the basis of such criteria as the production process, producers' sales and profits. If such separate identification of that production is not possible, the effects of the dumped imports shall be assessed by the examination of the production of the narrowest group or range of products, which includes the like product, for which the necessary information can be provided.

3.7 A determination of a threat of material injury shall be based on facts and not merely on allegation, conjecture or remote possibility. The change in circumstances which would create a situation in which the dumping would cause injury must be clearly foreseen and imminent. In making a determination regarding the existence of a threat of material injury, the authorities should consider, *inter alia*, such factors as:

(i) a significant rate of increase of dumped imports into the domestic market indicating the likelihood of substantially increased importation;

(ii) sufficient freely disposable, or an imminent, substantial increase in, capacity of the exporter indicating the likelihood of substantially increased dumped exports to the importing Member's market, taking into account the availability of other export markets to absorb any additional exports;

(iii) whether imports are entering at prices that will have a significant depressing or suppressing effect on domestic prices, and would likely increase demand for further imports; and

(iv) inventories of the product being investigated.

No one of these factors by itself can necessarily give decisive guidance but the totality of the factors considered must lead to the conclusion that further dumped exports are imminent and that, unless protective action is taken, material injury would occur.

3.8 With respect to cases where injury is threatened by dumped imports, the application of anti-dumping measures shall be considered and decided with special care.

Article 4: Definition of Domestic Industry

4.1   For the purposes of this Agreement, the term "domestic industry" shall be interpreted as referring to the domestic producers as a whole of the like products or to those of them whose collective output of the products constitutes a major proportion of the total domestic production of those products, except that:

(i)   when producers are related to the exporters or importers or are themselves importers of the allegedly dumped product, the term "domestic industry" may be interpreted as referring to the rest of the producers;

(ii)   in exceptional circumstances the territory of a Member may, for the production in question, be divided into two or more competitive markets and the producers within each market may be regarded as a separate industry if (a) the producers within such market sell all or almost all of their production of the product in question in that market, and (b) the demand in that market is not to any substantial degree supplied by producers of the product in question located elsewhere in the territory. In such circumstances, injury may be found to exist even where a major portion of the total domestic industry is not injured, provided there is a concentration of dumped imports into such an isolated market and provided further that the dumped imports are causing injury to the producers of all or almost all of the production within such market.

4.2   When the domestic industry has been interpreted as referring to the producers in a certain area, *i.e.* a market as defined in paragraph 1(ii), anti-dumping duties shall be levied only on the products in question consigned for final consumption to that area. When the constitutional law of the importing Member does not permit the levying of anti-dumping duties on such a basis, the importing Member may levy the anti-dumping duties without limitation only if (a) the exporters shall have been given an opportunity to cease exporting at dumped prices to the area concerned or otherwise give assurances pursuant to Article 8 and adequate assurances in this regard have not been promptly given, and (b) such duties cannot be levied only on products of specific producers which supply the area in question.

4.3 Where two or more countries have reached under the provisions of paragraph 8(a) of Article XXIV of GATT 1994 such a level of integration that they have the characteristics of a single, unified market, the industry in the entire area of integration shall be taken to be the domestic industry referred to in paragraph 1.

4.4 The provisions of paragraph 6 of Article 3 shall be applicable to this Article.

Article 5: Initiation and Subsequent Investigation

5.1 Except as provided for in paragraph 6, an investigation to determine the existence, degree and effect of any alleged dumping shall be initiated upon a written application by or on behalf of the domestic industry.

5.2 An application under paragraph 1 shall include evidence of (a) dumping, (b) injury within the meaning of Article VI of GATT 1994 as interpreted by this Agreement, and (c) a causal link between the dumped imports and the alleged injury. Simple assertion, un-substantiated by relevant evidence, cannot be considered sufficient to meet the requirements of this paragraph. The application shall contain such information as is reasonably available to the applicant on the following:

   (i) the identity of the applicant and a description of the volume and value of the domestic production of the like product by the applicant. Where a written application is made on behalf of the domestic industry, the application shall identify the industry on behalf of which the application is made by a list of all known domestic producers of the like product (or associations of domestic producers of the like product) and, to the extent possible, a description of the volume and value of domestic production of the like product accounted for by such producers;

   (ii) a complete description of the allegedly dumped product, the names of the country or countries of origin or export in question, the identity of each known exporter or foreign producer and a list of known persons importing the product in question;

(iii) information on prices at which the product in question is sold when destined for consumption in the domestic markets of the country or countries of origin or export (or, where appropriate, information on the prices at which the product is sold from the country or countries of origin or export to a third country or countries, or on the constructed value of the product) and information on export prices or, where appropriate, on the prices at which the product is first resold to an independent buyer in the territory of the importing Member;

(iv) information on the evolution of the volume of the allegedly dumped imports, the effect of these imports on prices of the like product in the domestic market and the consequent impact of the imports on the domestic industry, as demonstrated by relevant factors and indices having a bearing on the state of the domestic industry, such as those listed in paragraphs 2 and 4 of Article 3.

5.3 The authorities shall examine the accuracy and adequacy of the evidence provided in the application to determine whether there is sufficient evidence to justify the initiation of an investigation.

5.4 An investigation shall not be initiated pursuant to paragraph 1 unless the authorities have determined, on the basis of an examination of the degree of support for, or opposition to, the application expressed by domestic producers of the like product, that the application has been made by or on behalf of the domestic industry. The application shall be considered to have been made "by or on behalf of the domestic industry" if it is supported by those domestic producers whose collective output constitutes more than 50 per cent of the total production of the like product produced by that portion of the domestic industry expressing either support for or opposition to the application. However, no investigation shall be initiated when domestic producers expressly supporting the application account for less than 25 per cent of total production of the like product produced by the domestic industry.

5.5 The authorities shall avoid, unless a decision has been made to initiate an investigation, any publicising of the application for the initiation of an investigation. However, after receipt of a properly documented application and before proceeding to initiate an investigation, the authorities shall notify the government of the exporting Member concerned.

5.6 If, in special circumstances, the authorities concerned decide to initiate an investigation without having received a written application by or on behalf of a domestic industry for the initiation of such investigation, they shall proceed only if they have sufficient evidence of dumping, injury and a causal link, as described in paragraph 2, to justify the initiation of an investigation.

5.7 The evidence of both dumping and injury shall be considered simultaneously *(a)* in the decision whether or not to initiate an investigation, and *(b)* thereafter, during the course of the investigation, starting on a date not later than the earliest date on which in accordance with the provisions of this Agreement provisional measures may be applied.

5.8 An application under paragraph 1 shall be rejected and an investigation shall be terminated promptly as soon as the authorities concerned are satisfied that there is not sufficient evidence of either dumping or of injury to justify proceeding with the case. There shall be immediate termination in cases where the authorities determine that the margin of dumping is *de minimis*, or that the volume of dumped imports, actual or potential, or the injury, is negligible. The margin of dumping shall be considered to be *de minimis* if this margin is less than 2 per cent, expressed as a percentage of the export price. The volume of dumped imports shall normally be regarded as negligible if the volume of dumped imports from a particular country is found to account for less than 3 per cent of imports of the like product in the importing Member, unless countries which individually account for less than 3 per cent of the imports of the like product in the importing Member collectively account for more than 7 per cent of imports of the like product in the importing Member.

5.9 An anti-dumping proceeding shall not hinder the procedures of customs clearance.

5.10 Investigations shall, except in special circumstances, be concluded within one year, and in no case more than 18 months, after their initiation.

Article 6: Evidence

6.1   All interested parties in an anti-dumping investigation shall be given notice of the information which the authorities require and ample opportunity to present in writing all evidence which they consider relevant in respect of the investigation in question.

  6.1.1 Exporters or foreign producers receiving questionnaires used in an anti-dumping investigation shall be given at least 30 days for reply. Due consideration should be given to any request for an extension of the 30 day period and, upon cause shown, such an extension should be granted whenever practicable.

  6.1.2 Subject to the requirement to protect confidential information, evidence presented in writing by one interested party shall be made available promptly to other interested parties participating in the investigation.

  6.1.3 As soon as an investigation has been initiated, the authorities shall provide the full text of the written application received under paragraph 1 of Article 5 to the known exporters and to the authorities of the exporting Member and shall make it available, upon request, to other interested parties involved. Due regard shall be paid to the requirement for the protection of confidential information, as provided for in paragraph 5.

6.2   Throughout the anti-dumping investigation all interested parties shall have a full opportunity for the defence of their interests. To this end, the authorities shall, on request, provide opportunities for all interested parties to meet those parties with adverse interests, so that opposing views may be presented and rebuttal arguments offered. Provision of such opportunities must take account of the need to preserve confidentiality and of the convenience to the parties. There shall be no obligation on any party to attend a meeting, and failure to do so shall not be prejudicial to that party's case. Interested parties shall also have the right, on justification, to present other information orally.

6.3   Oral information provided under paragraph 2 shall be taken into account by the authorities only in so far as it is subsequently reproduced in writing and made available to other interested parties, as provided for in subparagraph 1.2.

6.4 The authorities shall whenever practicable provide timely opportunities for all interested parties to see all information that is relevant to the presentation of their cases, that is not confidential as defined in paragraph 5, and that is used by the authorities in an anti-dumping investigation, and to prepare presentations on the basis of this information.

6.5 Any information which is by nature confidential (for example, because its disclosure would be of significant competitive advantage to a competitor or because its disclosure would have a significantly adverse effect upon a person supplying the information or upon a person from whom that person acquired the information), or which is provided on a confidential basis by parties to an investigation shall, upon good cause shown, be treated as such by the authorities. Such information shall not be disclosed without specific permission of the party submitting it.

6.5.1 The authorities shall require interested parties providing confidential information to furnish non-confidential summaries thereof. These summaries shall be in sufficient detail to permit a reasonable understanding of the substance of the information submitted in confidence. In exceptional circumstances, such parties may indicate that such information is not susceptible of summary. In such exceptional circumstances, a statement of the reasons why summarisation is not possible must be provided.

6.5.2 If the authorities find that a request for confidentiality is not warranted and if the supplier of the information is either unwilling to make the information public or to authorise its disclosure in generalised or summary form, the authorities may disregard such information unless it can be demonstrated to their satisfaction from appropriate sources that the information is correct.

6.6 Except in circumstances provided for in paragraph 8, the authorities shall during the course of an investigation satisfy themselves as to the accuracy of the information supplied by interested parties upon which their findings are based.

6.7 In order to verify information provided or to obtain further details, the authorities may carry out investigations in the territory of other Members as required, provided they obtain the agreement of the firms concerned and notify the representatives of the government of the Member in question, and unless that Member objects to the investigation. The procedures described in Annex I shall apply to investigations carried out in the territory of other Members. Subject to the requirement to protect confidential information, the authorities shall make the results of any such investigations available, or shall provide disclosure thereof pursuant to paragraph 9, to the firms to which they pertain and may make such results available to the applicants.

6.8 In cases in which any interested party refuses access to, or otherwise does not provide, necessary information within a reasonable period or significantly impedes the investigation, preliminary and final determinations, affirmative or negative, may be made on the basis of the facts available. The provisions of Annex II shall be observed in the application of this paragraph.

6.9 The authorities shall, before a final determination is made, inform all interested parties of the essential facts under consideration which form the basis for the decision whether to apply definitive measures. Such disclosure should take place in sufficient time for the parties to defend their interests.

6.10 The authorities shall, as a rule, determine an individual margin of dumping for each known exporter or producer concerned of the product under investigation. In cases where the number of exporters, producers, importers or types of products involved is so large as to make such a determination impracticable, the authorities may limit their examination either to a reasonable number of interested parties or products by using samples which are statistically valid on the basis of information available to the authorities at the time of the selection, or to the largest percentage of the volume of the exports from the country in question which can reasonably be investigated.

  6.10.1 Any selection of exporters, producers, importers or types of products made under this paragraph shall preferably be chosen in consultation with and with the consent of the exporters, producers or importers concerned.

6.10.2 In cases where the authorities have limited their examination, as provided for in this paragraph, they shall nevertheless determine an individual margin of dumping for any exporter or producer not initially selected who submits the necessary information in time for that information to be considered during the course of the investigation, except where the number of exporters or producers is so large that individual examinations would be unduly burdensome to the authorities and prevent the timely completion of the investigation. Voluntary responses shall not be discouraged.

6.11 For the purposes of this Agreement, "interested parties" shall include:

(i) an exporter or foreign producer or the importer of a product subject to investigation, or a trade or business association a majority of the members of which are producers, exporters or importers of such product;

(ii) the government of the exporting Member; and

(iii) a producer of the like product in the importing Member or a trade and business association a majority of the Members of which produce the like product in the territory of the importing Member.

This list shall not preclude Members from allowing domestic or foreign parties other than those mentioned above to be included as interested parties.

6.12 The authorities shall provide opportunities for industrial users of the product under investigation, and for representative consumer organisations in cases where the product is commonly sold at the retail level, to provide information which is relevant to the investigation regarding dumping, injury and causality.

6.13 The authorities shall take due account of any difficulties experienced by interested parties, in particular small companies, in supplying information requested, and shall provide any assistance practicable.

6.14 The procedures set out above are not intended to prevent the authorities of a Member from proceeding expeditiously with regard to initiating an investigation, reaching preliminary or final determinations, whether affirmative or negative, or from applying provisional or final measures, in accordance with relevant provisions of this Agreement.

Article 7: Provisional Measures

7.1 Provisional measures may be applied only if:

(i)   an investigation has been initiated in accordance with the provisions of Article 5, a public notice has been given to that effect and interested parties have been given adequate opportunities to submit information and make comments;

(ii)   a preliminary affirmative determination has been made of dumping and consequent injury to a domestic industry; and

(iii) the authorities concerned judge such measures necessary to prevent injury being caused during the investigation.

7.2 Provisional measures may take the form of a provisional duty or, preferably, a security by cash deposit or bond equal to the amount of the anti-dumping duty provisionally estimated, being not greater than the provisionally estimated margin of dumping. Withholding of appraisement is an appropriate provisional measure, provided that the normal duty and the estimated amount of the anti-dumping duty be indicated and as long as the withholding of appraisement is subject to the same conditions as other provisional measures.

7.3 Provisional measures shall not be applied sooner than 60 days from the date of initiation of the investigation.

7.4 The application of provisional measures shall be limited to as short a period as possible, not exceeding four months or, on decision of the authorities concerned, upon request by exporters representing a significant percentage of the trade involved, to a period not exceeding six months. When authorities, in the course of an investigation, examine whether a duty lower than the margin of dumping would be sufficient to remove injury, these periods may be six and nine months, respectively.

7.5 The relevant provisions of Article 9 shall be followed in the application of provisional measures.

Article 8: Price Undertakings

8.1 Proceedings may be suspended or terminated without the imposition of provisional measures or anti-dumping duties upon receipt of satisfactory voluntary undertakings from any exporter to revise its prices or to cease exports to the area in question at dumped prices so that the authorities are satisfied that the injurious effect of the dumping is eliminated. Price increases under such undertakings shall not be higher than necessary to eliminate the margin of dumping. It is desirable that the price increases be less than the margin of dumping if such increases would be adequate to remove the injury to the domestic industry.

8.2 Price undertakings shall not be sought or accepted from exporters unless the authorities of the importing Member have made a preliminary affirmative determination of dumping and injury caused by such dumping.

8.3 Undertakings offered need not be accepted if the authorities consider their acceptance impractical, for example, if the number of actual or potential exporters is too great, or for other reasons, including reasons of general policy. Should the case arise and where practicable, the authorities shall provide to the exporter the reasons which have led them to consider acceptance of an undertaking as inappropriate, and shall, to the extent possible, give the exporter an opportunity to make comments thereon.

8.4 If an undertaking is accepted, the investigation of dumping and injury shall nevertheless be completed if the exporter so desires or the authorities so decide. In such a case, if a negative determination of dumping or injury is made, the undertaking shall automatically lapse, except in cases where such a determination is due in large part to the existence of a price undertaking. In such cases, the authorities may require that an undertaking be maintained for a reasonable period consistent with the provisions of this Agreement. In the event that an affirmative determination of dumping and injury is made, the undertaking shall continue consistent with its terms and the provisions of this Agreement.

8.5 Price undertakings may be suggested by the authorities of the importing Member, but no exporter shall be forced to enter into such undertakings. The fact that exporters do not offer such undertakings, or do not accept an invitation to do so, shall in no way prejudice the consideration of the case. However, the authorities are free to determine that a threat of injury is more likely to be realised if the dumped imports continue.

8.6 Authorities of an importing Member may require any exporter from whom an undertaking has been accepted to provide periodically information relevant to the fulfilment of such an undertaking and to permit verification of pertinent data. In case of violation of an undertaking, the authorities of the importing Member may take, under this Agreement in conformity with its provisions, expeditious actions which may constitute immediate application of provisional measures using the best information available. In such cases, definitive duties may be levied in accordance with this Agreement on products entered for consumption not more than 90 days before the application of such provisional measures, except that any such retroactive assessment shall not apply to imports entered before the violation of the undertaking.

Article 9: Imposition and Collection of Anti-Dumping Duties

9.1 The decision whether or not to impose an anti-dumping duty in cases where all requirements for the imposition have been fulfilled, and the decision whether the amount of the anti-dumping duty to be imposed shall be the full margin of dumping or less, are decisions to be made by the authorities of the importing Member. It is desirable that the imposition be permissive in the territory of all Members, and that the duty be less than the margin if such lesser duty would be adequate to remove the injury to the domestic industry.

9.2 When an anti-dumping duty is imposed in respect of any product, such anti-dumping duty shall be collected in the appropriate amounts in each case, on a non-discriminatory basis on imports of such product from all sources found to be dumped and causing injury, except as to imports from those sources from which price undertakings under the terms of this Agreement have been accepted. The authorities shall name the supplier or suppliers of the product concerned. If, however, several suppliers from the same country are involved, and it is impracticable to name all these suppliers, the authorities may name the supplying country concerned. If several suppliers from more than one country are involved, the authorities may name either all the suppliers involved, or, if this is impracticable, all the supplying countries involved.

9.3 The amount of the anti-dumping duty shall not exceed the margin of dumping as established under Article 2.

9.3.1 When the amount of the anti-dumping duty is assessed on a retrospective basis, the determination of the final liability for payment of anti-dumping duties shall take place as soon as possible, normally within 12 months, and in no case more than 18 months, after the date on which a request for a final assessment of the amount of the anti-dumping duty has been made. Any refund shall be made promptly and normally in not more than 90 days following the determination of final liability made pursuant to this sub-paragraph. In any case, where a refund is not made within 90 days, the authorities shall provide an explanation if so requested.

9.3.2 When the amount of the anti-dumping duty is assessed on a prospective basis, provision shall be made for a prompt refund, upon request, of any duty paid in excess of the margin of dumping. A refund of any such duty paid in excess of the actual margin of dumping shall normally take place within 12 months, and in no case more than 18 months, after the date on which a request for a refund, duly supported by evidence, has been made by an importer of the product subject to the anti-dumping duty. The refund authorised should normally be made within 90 days of the above noted decision.

9.3.3 In determining whether and to what extent a reimbursement should be made when the export price is constructed in accordance with paragraph 3 of Article 2, authorities should take account of any change in normal value, any change in costs incurred between importation and resale, and any movement in the resale price which is duly reflected in subsequent selling prices, and should calculate the export price with no deduction for the amount of anti-dumping duties paid when conclusive evidence of the above is provided.

9.4 When the authorities have limited their examination in accordance with the second sentence of paragraph 10 of Article 6, any anti-dumping duty applied to imports from exporters or producers not included in the examination shall not exceed:

(i) the weighted average margin of dumping established with respect to the selected exporters or producers, or,

(ii) where the liability for payment of anti-dumping duties is calculated on the basis of a prospective normal value, the difference between the weighted average normal value of the selected exporters or producers and the export prices of exporters or producers not individually examined, provided that the authorities shall disregard for the purpose of this paragraph any zero and *de minimis* margins and margins established under the circumstances referred to in paragraph 8 of Article 6. The authorities shall apply individual duties or normal values to imports from any exporter or producer not included in the examination who has provided the necessary information during the course of the investigation, as provided for in sub-paragraph 10.2 of Article 6.

9.5 If a product is subject to anti-dumping duties in an importing Member, the authorities shall promptly carry out a review for the purpose of determining individual margins of dumping for any exporters or producers in the exporting country in question who have not exported the product to the importing Member during the period of investigation, provided that these exporters or producers can show that they are not related to any of the exporters or producers in the exporting country who are subject to the anti-dumping duties on the product. Such a review shall be initiated and carried out on an accelerated basis, compared to normal duty assessment and review proceedings in the importing Member. No anti-dumping duties shall be levied on imports from such exporters or producers while the review is being carried out. The authorities may, however, withhold appraisement and/or request guarantees to ensure that, should such a review result in a determination of dumping in respect of such producers or exporters, anti-dumping duties can be levied retroactively to the date of the initiation of the review.

Article 10: Retroactivity

10.1 Provisional measures and anti-dumping duties shall only be applied to products which enter for consumption after the time when the decision taken under paragraph 1 of Article 7 and paragraph 1 of Article 9, respectively, enters into force, subject to the exceptions set out in this Article.

10.2 Where a final determination of injury (but not of a threat thereof or of a material retardation of the establishment of an industry) is made or, in the case of a final determination of a threat of injury, where the effect of the dumped imports would, in the absence of the provisional measures, have led to a determination of injury, anti-dumping duties may be levied retroactively for the period for which provisional measures, if any, have been applied.

10.3 If the definitive anti-dumping duty is higher than the provisional duty paid or payable, or the amount estimated for the purpose of the security, the difference shall not be collected. If the definitive duty is lower than the provisional duty paid or payable, or the amount estimated for the purpose of the security, the difference shall be reimbursed or the duty recalculated, as the case may be.

10.4 Except as provided in paragraph 2, where a determination of threat of injury or material retardation is made (but no injury has yet occurred) a definitive anti-dumping duty may be imposed only from the date of the determination of threat of injury or material retardation, and any cash deposit made during the period of the application of provisional measures shall be refunded and any bonds released in an expeditious manner.

10.5 Where a final determination is negative, any cash deposit made during the period of the application of provisional measures shall be refunded and any bonds released in an expeditious manner.

10.6 A definitive anti-dumping duty may be levied on products which were entered for consumption not more than 90 days prior to the date of application of provisional measures, when the authorities determine for the dumped product in question that:

(i)   there is a history of dumping which caused injury or that the importer was, or should have been, aware that the exporter practises dumping and that such dumping would cause injury, and

(ii)   the injury is caused by massive dumped imports of a product in a relatively short time which in light of the timing and the volume of the dumped imports and other circumstances (such as a rapid build up of inventories of the imported product) is likely to seriously undermine the remedial effect of the definitive anti-dumping duty to be applied, provided that the importers concerned have been given an opportunity to comment.

10.7 The authorities may, after initiating an investigation, take such measures as the withholding of appraisement or assessment as may be necessary to collect anti-dumping duties retroactively, as provided for in paragraph 6, once they have sufficient evidence that the conditions set forth in that paragraph are satisfied.

10.8 No duties shall be levied retroactively pursuant to paragraph 6 on products entered for consumption prior to the date of initiation of the investigation.

Article 11: Duration and Review of Anti-Dumping Duties and Price Undertakings

11.1 An anti-dumping duty shall remain in force only as long as and to the extent necessary to counteract dumping which is causing injury.

11.2 The authorities shall review the need for the continued imposition of the duty, where warranted, on their own initiative or, provided that a reasonable period of time has elapsed since the imposition of the definitive anti-dumping duty, upon request by any interested party which submits positive information substantiating the need for a review. Interested parties shall have the right to request the authorities to examine whether the continued imposition of the duty is necessary to offset dumping, whether the injury would be likely to continue or recur if the duty were removed or varied, or both. If, as a result of the review under this paragraph, the authorities determine that the anti-dumping duty is no longer warranted, it shall be terminated immediately.

11.3 Notwithstanding the provisions of paragraphs 1 and 2, any definitive anti-dumping duty shall be terminated on a date not later than five years from its imposition (or from the date of the most recent review under paragraph 2 if that review has covered both dumping and injury, or under this paragraph), unless the authorities determine, in a review initiated before that date on their own initiative or upon a duly substantiated request made by or on behalf of the domestic industry within a reasonable period of time prior to that date, that the expiry of the duty would be likely to lead to continuation or recurrence of dumping and injury. The duty may remain in force pending the outcome of such a review.

11.4 The provisions of Article 6 regarding evidence and procedure shall apply to any review carried out under this Article. Any such review shall be carried out expeditiously and shall normally be concluded within 12 months of the date of initiation of the review.

11.5 The provisions of this Article shall apply *mutatis mutandis* to price undertakings accepted under Article 8.

Article 12: Public Notice and Explanation of Determinations

12.1 When the authorities are satisfied that there is sufficient evidence to justify the initiation of an anti-dumping investigation pursuant to Article 5, the Member or Members, the products of which are subject to such investigation and other interested parties known to the investigating authorities to have an interest therein shall be notified and a public notice shall be given.

12.1.1 A public notice of the initiation of an investigation shall contain, or otherwise make available through a separate report, adequate information on the following:

(i)   the name of the exporting country or countries and the product involved;

(ii) the date of initiation of the investigation;

(iii) the basis on which dumping is alleged in the application;

(iv) a summary of the factors on which the allegation of injury is based;

(v)   the address to which representations by interested parties should be directed;

(vi) the timelimits allowed to interested parties for making their views known.

12.2 Public notice shall be given of any preliminary or final determination, whether affirmative or negative, of any decision to accept an undertaking pursuant to Article 8, of the termination of such an undertaking, and of the termination of a definitive anti-dumping duty. Each such notice shall set forth, or otherwise make available through a separate report, in sufficient detail the findings and conclusions reached on all issues of fact and law considered material by the investigating authorities. All such notices and reports shall be forwarded to the Member or Members, the products of which are subject to such determination or undertaking and to other interested parties known to have an interest therein.

12.2.1 A public notice of the imposition of provisional measures shall set forth, or otherwise make available through a separate report, sufficiently detailed explanations for the preliminary determinations on dumping and injury and shall refer to the matters of fact and law which have led to arguments being accepted or rejected. Such a notice or report shall, due regard being paid to the requirement for the protection of confidential information, contain in particular:

(i)   the names of the suppliers, or when this is impracticable, the supplying countries involved;

(ii)   a description of the product which is sufficient for customs purposes;

(iii) the margins of dumping established and a full explanation of the reasons for the methodology used in the establishment and comparison of the export price and the normal value under Article 2;

(iv)   considerations relevant to the injury determination as set out in Article 3;

(v)   the main reasons leading to the determination.

12.2.2 A public notice of conclusion or suspension of an investigation in the case of an affirmative determination providing for the imposition of a definitive duty or the acceptance of a price undertaking shall contain, or otherwise make available through a separate report, all relevant information on the matters of fact and law and reasons which have led to the imposition of final measures or the acceptance of a price undertaking, due regard being paid to the requirement for the protection of confidential information. In particular, the notice or report shall contain the information described in subparagraph 2.1, as well as the reasons for the acceptance or rejection of relevant arguments or claims made by the exporters and importers, and the basis for any decision made under sub-paragraph 10.2 of Article 6.

12.2.3 A public notice of the termination or suspension of an investigation following the acceptance of an undertaking pursuant to Article 8 shall include, or otherwise make available through a separate report, the non-confidential part of this undertaking.

12.3 The provisions of this Article shall apply *mutatis mutandis* to the initiation and completion of reviews pursuant to Article 11 and to decisions under Article 10 to apply duties retroactively.

Article 13: Judicial Review

Each Member whose national legislation contains provisions on anti-dumping measures shall maintain judicial, arbitral or administrative tribunals or procedures for the purpose, *inter alia*, of the prompt review of administrative actions relating to final determinations and reviews of determinations within the meaning of Article 11. Such tribunals or procedures shall be independent of the authorities responsible for the determination or review in question.

Article 14: Anti-Dumping Action on Behalf of a Third Country

14.1 An application for anti-dumping action on behalf of a third country shall be made by the authorities of the third country requesting action.

14.2 Such an application shall be supported by price information to show that the imports are being dumped and by detailed information to show that the alleged dumping is causing injury to the domestic industry concerned in the third country. The government of the third country shall afford all assistance to the authorities of the importing country to obtain any further information which the latter may require.

14.3 In considering such an application, the authorities of the importing country shall consider the effects of the alleged dumping on the industry concerned as a whole in the third country; that is to say, the injury shall not be assessed in relation only to the effect of the alleged dumping on the industry's exports to the importing country or even on the industry's total exports.

14.4 The decision whether or not to proceed with a case shall rest with the importing country. If the importing country decides that it is prepared to take action, the initiation of the approach to the Council for Trade in Goods seeking its approval for such action shall rest with the importing country.

Article 15: Developing Country Members

It is recognised that special regard must be given by developed country Members to the special situation of developing country Members when considering the application of anti-dumping measures under this Agreement. Possibilities of constructive remedies provided for by this Agreement shall be explored before applying anti-dumping duties where they would affect the essential interests of developing country Members.

PART II

Article 16: Committee on Anti-Dumping Practices

16.1 There is hereby established a Committee on Anti-Dumping Practices (referred to in this Agreement as the "Committee") composed of representatives from each of the Members. The Committee shall elect its own Chairman and shall meet not less than twice a year and otherwise as envisaged by relevant provisions of this Agreement at the request of any Member. The Committee shall carry out responsibilities as assigned to it under this Agreement or by the Members and it shall afford Members the opportunity of consulting on any matters relating to the operation of the Agreement or the furtherance of its objectives. The WTO Secretariat shall act as the Secretariat to the Committee.

16.2 The Committee may set up subsidiary bodies as appropriate.

16.3 In carrying out their functions, the Committee and any subsidiary bodies may consult with and seek information from any source they deem appropriate. However, before the Committee or a subsidiary body seeks such information from a source within the jurisdiction of a Member, it shall inform the Member involved. It shall obtain the consent of the Member and any firm to be consulted.

16.4 Members shall report without delay to the Committee all preliminary or final anti-dumping actions taken. Such reports shall be available in the Secretariat for inspection by other Members. Members shall also submit, on a semi-annual basis, reports of any anti-dumping actions taken within the preceding six months. The semi-annual reports shall be submitted on an agreed standard form.

16.5 Each Member shall notify the Committee, *(a)* which of its authorities are competent to initiate and conduct investigations referred to in Article 5, and *(b)* its domestic procedures governing the initiation and conduct of such investigations.

Article 17: Consultation and Dispute Settlement

17.1 Except as otherwise provided herein, the Dispute Settlement Understanding is applicable to consultations and the settlement of disputes under this Agreement.

17.2 Each Member shall afford sympathetic consideration to, and shall afford adequate opportunity for consultation regarding, representations made by another Member with respect to any matter affecting the operation of this Agreement.

17.3 If any Member considers that any benefit accruing to it, directly or indirectly, under this Agreement is being nullified or impaired, or that the achievement of any objective is being impeded, by another Member or Members, it may, with a view to reaching a mutually satisfactory resolution of the matter, request in writing consultations with the Member or Members in question. Each Member shall afford sympathetic consideration to any request from another Member for consultation.

17.4 If the Member that requested consultations considers that the consultations pursuant to paragraph 3 have failed to achieve a mutually agreed solution, and if final action has been taken by the administering authorities of the importing Member to levy definitive anti-dumping duties or to accept price undertakings, it may refer the matter to the Dispute Settlement Body ("DSB"). When a provisional measure has a significant impact and the Member that requested consultations considers that the measure was taken contrary to the provisions of paragraph 1 of Article 7, that Member may also refer such matter to the DSB.

17.5 The DSB shall, at the request of the complaining party, establish a panel to examine the matter based upon:

(i) a written statement of the Member making the request indicating how a benefit accruing to it, directly or indirectly, under this Agreement has been nullified or impaired, or that the achieving of the objectives of the Agreement is being impeded, and

(ii) the facts made available in conformity with appropriate domestic procedures to the authorities of the importing Member.

17.6 In examining the matter referred to in paragraph 5:

> (i)   in its assessment of the facts of the matter, the panel shall determine whether the authorities' establishment of the facts was proper and whether their evaluation of those facts was unbiased and objective. If the establishment of the facts was proper and the evaluation was unbiased and objective, even though the panel might have reached a different conclusion, the evaluation shall not be overturned;

> (ii)   the panel shall interpret the relevant provisions of the Agreement in accordance with customary rules of interpretation of public international law. Where the panel finds that a relevant provision of the Agreement admits of more than one permissible interpretation, the panel shall find the authorities' measure to be in conformity with the Agreement if it rests upon one of those permissible interpretations.

17.7 Confidential information provided to the panel shall not be disclosed without formal authorisation from the person, body or authority providing such information. Where such information is requested from the panel but release of such information by the panel is not authorised, a non-confidential summary of the information, authorised by the person, body or authority providing the information, shall be provided.

PART III

Article 18: Final Provisions

18.1 No specific action against dumping of exports from another Member can be taken except in accordance with the provisions of GATT 1994, as interpreted by this Agreement.

18.2 Reservations may not be entered in respect of any of the provisions of this Agreement without the consent of the other Members.

18.3 Subject to sub-paragraphs 3.1 and 3.2, the provisions of this Agreement shall apply to investigations, and reviews of existing measures, initiated pursuant to applications which have been made on or after the date of entry into force for a Member of the WTO Agreement.

18.3.1 With respect to the calculation of margins of dumping in refund procedures under paragraph 3 of Article 9, the rules used in the most recent determination or review of dumping shall apply.

18.3.2 For the purposes of paragraph 3 of Article 11, existing anti-dumping measures shall be deemed to be imposed on a date not later than the date of entry into force for a Member of the WTO Agreement, except in cases in which the domestic legislation of a Member in force on that date already included a clause of the type provided for in that paragraph.

18.4 Each Member shall take all necessary steps, of a general or particular character, to ensure, not later than the date of entry into force of the WTO Agreement for it, the conformity of its laws, regulations and administrative procedures with the provisions of this Agreement as they may apply for the Member in question.

18.5 Each Member shall inform the Committee of any changes in its laws and regulations relevant to this Agreement and in the administration of such laws and regulations.

18.6 The Committee shall review annually the implementation and operation of this Agreement taking into account the objectives thereof. The Committee shall inform annually the Council for Trade in Goods of developments during the period covered by such reviews.

18.7 The Annexes to this Agreement constitute an integral part thereof.

ANNEX I: Procedures for ON-THE-SPOT Investigations Pursuant to Paragraph 7 of Article 6

1. Upon initiation of an investigation, the authorities of the exporting Member and the firms known to be concerned should be informed of the intention to carry out on the spot investigations.

2. If in exceptional circumstances it is intended to include non-governmental experts in the investigating team, the firms and the authorities of the exporting Member should be so

informed. Such non-governmental experts should be subject to effective sanctions for breach of confidentiality requirements.

3. It should be standard practice to obtain explicit agreement of the firms concerned in the exporting Member before the visit is finally scheduled.

4. As soon as the agreement of the firms concerned has been obtained, the investigating authorities should notify the authorities of the exporting Member of the names and addresses of the firms to be visited and the dates agreed.

5. Sufficient advance notice should be given to the firms in question before the visit is made.

6. Visits to explain the questionnaire should only be made at the request of an exporting firm. Such a visit may only be made if *(a)* the authorities of the importing Member notify the representatives of the Member in question, and *(b)* the latter do not object to the visit.

7. As the main purpose of the on the spot investigation is to verify information provided or to obtain further details, it should be carried out after the response to the questionnaire has been received unless the firm agrees to the contrary and the government of the exporting Member is informed by the investigating authorities of the anticipated visit and does not object to it; further, it should be standard practice prior to the visit to advise the firms concerned of the general nature of the information to be verified and of any further information which needs to be provided, though this should not preclude requests to be made on the spot for further details to be provided in the light of information obtained.

8. Enquiries or questions put by the authorities or firms of the exporting Members and essential to a successful on the spot investigation should, whenever possible, be answered before the visit is made.

Annex II: Best Information
Available in Terms of Paragraph 8 of Article 6

1. As soon as possible after the initiation of the investigation, the investigating authorities should specify in detail the information required from any interested party, and the

manner in which that information should be structured by the interested party in its response. The authorities should also ensure that the party is aware that if information is not supplied within a reasonable time, the authorities will be free to make determinations on the basis of the facts available, including those contained in the application for the initiation of the investigation by the domestic industry.

2. The authorities may also request that an interested party provide its response in a particular medium (*e.g.* computer tape) or computer language. Where such a request is made, the authorities should consider the reasonable ability of the interested party to respond in the preferred medium or computer language, and should not request the party to use for its response a computer system other than that used by the party. The authority should not maintain a request for a computerised response if the interested party does not maintain computerised accounts and if presenting the response as requested would result in an unreasonable extra burden on the interested party, *e.g.* it would entail unreasonable additional cost and trouble. The authorities should not maintain a request for a response in a particular medium or computer language if the interested party does not maintain its computerised accounts in such medium or computer language and if presenting the response as requested would result in an unreasonable extra burden on the interested party, *e.g.* it would entail unreasonable additional cost and trouble.

3. All information which is verifiable, which is appropriately submitted so that it can be used in the investigation without undue difficulties, which is supplied in a timely fashion, and, where applicable, which is supplied in a medium or computer language requested by the authorities, should be taken into account when determinations are made. If a party does not respond in the preferred medium or computer language but the authorities find that the circumstances set out in paragraph 2 have been satisfied, the failure to respond in the preferred medium or computer language should not be considered to significantly impede the investigation.

4. Where the authorities do not have the ability to process information if provided in a particular medium (e.g. computer

tape), the information should be supplied in the form of written material or any other form acceptable to the authorities.

5. Even though the information provided may not be ideal in all respects, this should not justify the authorities from disregarding it, provided the interested party has acted to the best of its ability.

6. If evidence or information is not accepted, the supplying party should be informed forthwith of the reasons therefor, and should have an opportunity to provide further explanations within a reasonable period, due account being taken of the timelimits of the investigation. If the explanations are considered by the authorities as not being satisfactory, the reasons for the rejection of such evidence or information should be given in any published determinations.

7. If the authorities have to base their findings, including those with respect to normal value, on information from a secondary source, including the information supplied in the application for the initiation of the investigation, they should do so with special circumspection. In such cases, the authorities should, where practicable, check the information from other independent sources at their disposal, such as published price lists, official import statistics and customs returns, and from the information obtained from other interested parties during the investigation. It is clear, however, that if an interested party does not cooperate and, thus, relevant information is being withheld from the authorities, this situation could lead to a result which is less favourable to the party than if the party did cooperate.

Liberty Institute

Liberty Institute is an independent think-tank dedicated to empowering the people by harnessing the power of the market. It seeks to build understanding and appreciation of the four institutional pillars of a free society — *Individual Rights, Rule of Law, Limited Government* and *Free Market.*

The Institute undertakes a number of activities, among them research and advocacy on public policy issues. It organises conferences, and has a growing publications programme. At present, the Institute's core areas of interest include development economics, education, environment, health, security, and trade.

The Institute was established in 1996 as a non-profit organisation. It solicits the support of all freedom loving individuals and organisations. It strives to retain its independence, demonstrate its commitment, and live up to its motto: *"Where the mind is without fear..."*

LIBERTY INSTITUTE
Julian L. Simon Centre, C-4/8, Sahyadri, Plot 5, Sector 12, Dwarka, New Delhi 110 045. India
Tel: 91-11-25079214. Fax: 91-11-25079101. Email: info@libertyindia.org, liberty@nda.vsnl.net.in
Websites: www.libertyindia.org, www.indianelections2004.org

Rajiv Gandhi Institute for Contemporary Studies

The Rajiv Gandhi Institute for Contemporary Studies (RGICS), New Delhi is part of the Rajiv Gandhi Foundation and functions as a think tank. The target audience of the RGICS includes parliamentarians, legislators and representatives of political parties, public policymakers and their advisers, the intelligentsia, the media and various interest groups. To interface with these groups, RGICS uses different modes of communication like books, monographs, working papers, symposia, discussions, talks and lectures. The RGICS research work is focused on international economic relations, law reforms, IT and economic reforms in India.

RAJIV GANDHI INSTITUTE FOR CONTEMPORARY STUDIES,
Rajiv Gandhi Foundation, Jawahar Bhawan, Dr. Rajendra Prasad Road, New Delhi - 110001. India.
Tel: 91-11-23312456, 23755117. Fax: 91-11-23755119. Web-Add-http://www.rgfindia.com